My Forever Friend

He Makes the Impossible, Possible

9-29-07

To Millie & Gordon Roberts,

Enjoy! My prayer is that my book will be a blessing to you. Share it with all you can.

God Bless you.

Roen A. Wilson

My Forever Friend

FIRST EDITION
Copyright © 2007 by
Roen A. Wilson

Cover illustration and book design by MacMouser Graphics, Portland Oregon, http://www.macmouser.com

Life*Scape* Publishing

19291 SE 502ⁿᵈ Avenue
Sandy OR 97055
503-668-7956

ISBN 978-0-9786141-26   PRINTED IN U.S.A.

My
Forever Friend

Preface

Someone who apparently didn't know any better said, "I will bless the Lord at all times, His praise shall continually be in my mouth." I mean, what if that really worked? Come to think of it, we don't get very far into the Bible story before we discover that it seems to be a Scripture principle—that we praise Him in the good times and in the not-so-good times. Maybe King David, who wrote that statement above, was on to something.

My friend, Roen Wilson, learned this powerful reality early in life from her great God, and it changed everything for her. Faced by circumstances that could have destroyed her, she decided to take God at His Word and believe it when He said, "The joy of the Lord is my strength." She reasoned, "I need to be strong through this, and if strength comes from electing to have a joyous journey with God, then that's what I'll do."

Roen inspires me. For many years I've watched the beautiful outcome of her decision to trust God in every circumstance. Her retelling of the story will bless you, too. It smacks strongly of triumph. But Roen will be the first to tell you that she is not the hero of this book; the Hero is her strong God. As you walk with her through the pages she has created, you'll see.

Ruthie Jacobsen

1987-1994: Director, Women's Ministries, Oregon Conference

1995-Present: Director, Prayer Ministries, North American Division

Author of 10 books, including *God Wants to Hear You Sing*, published in 2007

My Forever Friend

In Search of Love

Book 1

Chapter 1

Doesn't Anybody Want Me?

The dream of "happily ever after" had evaporated, and my mother, Bernice, and father, Alfred, had decided to split up. They were living in Mountain View, California, at the time with their firstborn daughter, three-year-old Cathie (I had not yet arrived on the scene). In later years I learned that they had been quarreling about almost everything—Mother wanted to finish her education; Daddy didn't see why a woman needed to go to school. Daddy went to his lodge; Mother didn't approve. Daddy attended vaudeville shows; Mother wanted to go to church.

They'd married four years before, when she was only sixteen and feeling trapped by a harsh and demanding father who showed no affection for anyone in the family. He'd rant and shout at his six children to work harder and produce more, while doing little real work himself. So Mother, the eldest, left home for a "better man." But now Daddy had become a disappointment. Why did he go to vaudeville shows where scantily clad women danced on the stage? And why did he look at other women with such hunger?

Daddy came from a family of laborers and merchants and now worked as a carpenter. He had built the small house in which they lived.

1928

Mother and Daddy finally agreed to live separate lives under one roof, since Mother could not afford to move to another house. Interestingly enough, it was during this "separation" that Mother became pregnant.

Soon, however, Daddy and she filed for a divorce, but with the stipulation that Cathie would live with each of them every-other year. On this they agreed—they both deeply loved Cathie and wanted the best for her in both of their lives. No agreement, however, was made in the divorce papers regarding the unborn child.

After the divorce, Mother and Cathie traveled north to her parents' home in western Washington State. Mother's sister Gertie had enrolled at Walla Walla College, and when she left for Eastern Washington, Mother and Cathie accompanied her. They rented a house near the post office on the main street in College Place, a good location for the sewing business Mother planned to start. Somehow they would eke out a living—and they did.

When the year was up, Daddy came to Washington to claim Cathie, but Mother would not let her go. I was six months old, and Daddy and Mother finally reached a compromise in which she and I could accompany him back to California—in fact, could live with him again—at least during his year with Cathie.

I went along as extra baggage to live in a home that had little love. Cathie clearly resembled Daddy's family, but I looked different—more like my mother and her side of the family. In Daddy's eyes, I was an outcast.

1931

The Great Depression shut down Daddy's work in California, but mining in Montana still offered employment. So when I was ten months old, Daddy, Mother, and we two girls moved to Montana. Daddy started up his own business—a doughnut shop for the mining clientele. Then, when I was two-and-a-half years old, baby brother Alfred arrived. Since he was named after Daddy, to avoid confusion we called him Al. Four months after Al's birth, Mother and Daddy remarried.

But in 1931 the mines closed and the doughnut shop lost customers as the men moved away. So Mother and Daddy decided to return to

California and open a doughnut shop there. Daddy rented a small store in Oakland with a flat above, where we lived.

Cathie babysat Al and me when she was not in school, but otherwise I cared for little Al myself. My four-year-old heart hungered for approval. Anything my mother told me to do I tried hard to do right. Al kept me busy, but I loved him and wanted to keep him happy. Mother worked downstairs in the shop in the mornings and returned around noon for lunch. Then she'd go back to work and Al and I would be alone again until Cathie came home.

One morning Mother started the washing machine and left it running while she went downstairs to work. After Cathie left for school, I decided I could help Mother by putting the clothes from the machine into the rinse water. I'd watched Mother do it so many times, I felt sure I could do it to help her. How surprised she'd be, how pleased. Maybe she would even tell me what a good girl I was!

So after the machine had run for a long time, I turned the switch to stop the agitator and pulled two or three of my brother's diapers from the soapy water and reached toward the wringer. The clothes went through the wringer and dropped into the rinse water, just as they did when Mother washed. I pushed more clothes toward the moving rollers.

But as I reached toward the machine, Al dropped something and I turned to see if he was all right. Just then the rollers caught both the clothes and my fingers and dragged them into their jaws. I pulled with all my might, but the rollers would not let go. The wringers slowly pulled my hand—then my arm—as far as my arm would go. Al and I both began screaming.

Suddenly through the tumult I heard the door to the kitchen open, and I knew I was in bad trouble. Mother rushed into the house and hit the release bar on the machine, loosening the wringers enough so I could pull out my arm. But she was furious and began pushing and slapping me, shouting about all the trouble I had caused her during my short life. My arm ached terribly, but my heart was broken.

She left to get Daddy, as I whimpered. My arm throbbed terribly, but this was nothing compared with the heartache of her rejection.

As Daddy and Mother came up the stairs, I heard them arguing about who should carry me downstairs to the car. Finally Daddy lifted me in his arms, but I felt no love as he carried me to the car and later up the stairs to the hospital.

A doctor examined me and found no broken bones, but my throbbing arm hurt so badly, I yearned to cry. If I did, however, there would be bad trouble. Mother and Daddy continued trading angry words about my accident, adding to my quiet anguish. At church I'd heard about Jesus and how He always loves us and will help us if we ask. I now talked to Him and found comfort. I didn't really have anyone else. He was my only source of encouragement.

1932

The little doughnut shop failed. Between their quarrels I heard Mother talking to Daddy about the advantages of giving me away to some church friends who wanted a daughter. I knew the family was a good one and had a son, but I didn't want to leave my own family. Nonetheless, mother allowed the couple and their son to take me home with them to get to know me better and see if I would fit into their family. I called the woman Aunt Ruth. Her husband, Uncle Leslie, told me he thought it would be good for their son to have a sister. Another time Aunt Ruth took me grocery shopping with her and once to the Goodwill store.

At church, I loved the children's program. I sat quietly on my little chair and listened to the Bible stories. I learned to sing. "Jesus Loves Me" became my favorite song, and I learned memory verses quickly. I loved to watch the woman pumping the pedals on the little, brown organ in the corner. The song, "Jesus Loves the Little Children of the World" caught my attention, because as we sang the teacher would hold up pictures of children from other parts of the world. The picture of the little Dutch girl with her little, white hat, long skirt, apron, and wooden shoes fascinated me. I knew my great-grandfather had come from Holland. I loved to imagine what it would be like to go to church with children in their traditional dress and sit with them on Jesus' lap. The Dutch girl became my anchor.

Mother now avoided all conversation with me. If I came into a room where she and Cathie were talking, she would tell me to get out and mind my own business. She was apparently too busy for me, and our communication consisted of her giving me orders to care for Al and do other chores. I felt pushed away, but Aunt Ruth paid attention to me. I liked sitting on her lap.

Mother and Daddy's quarrels grew from screaming to hitting. Finally Mother decided to take us children and go home to her parents, and she asked Uncle Leslie and Aunt Ruth to drive us to Washington, where her parents lived. Daddy offered to let Uncle Leslie drive us north in his big, shiny, black town car, with its glass partition between the front and back seats. I sat with Aunt Ruth in front and Al sat in back with Mother and eight-year-old Cathie. Uncle Leslie drove. *Uncle Leslie and Aunt Ruth must have talked things over with Mother. Perhaps they planned to take me back with them to California. . .* I knew Mother was still talking about giving me to Aunt Ruth and Uncle Leslie. Mother didn't want me, but I thought Aunt Ruth did.

We had been driving most of a day when suddenly a drunk man ran out in front of the car. To miss him Uncle Leslie swerved and hit a tree, head on. Aunt Ruth pushed me to the floor of the car so I wouldn't get hurt, but the impact sent Mother through the glass between the front and back seats, knocking out six of her front teeth and badly cutting her face. Blood splattered everywhere. Mother had been lying down on the back seat, holding my brother. Cathie had been seated on the floor next to a pot of cooked beans. When the car crashed, the beans spilled all over her, leaving her lying on the floor crying. I heard Mother and the baby screaming. Aunt Ruth jumped out of the car and handed some diapers to Mother to hold over her face. I asked Jesus right away: "Please, take care of Mother. Please help her not to hurt so much."

Somebody in a Model A coupe stopped and offered to take us to a hospital. Mother rode in the front seat with the driver, and all three of us children occupied the outdoor rumble seat in the back. I wondered if Mother was going to die. Cathie hung on to Baby Al, and I remember feeling the wind as we drove. I liked that feeling. I sat back in my seat and begged Jesus to take care of Mother.

When we got to the hospital, staff members took us children into one examining room and Mother to a different one. A doctor found that we children were unhurt, and a kind nurse brought us each a drink of water and told us Mother would be a little while longer. Three hours later Mother's face had been stitched up and the bleeding in her mouth stopped. Aunt Ruth and Uncle Leslie came to get us in a car, and I nestled into Aunt Ruth's side. Cathie and Al sat in the back seat, with Mother in-between.

Uncle Leslie drove us to a cottage not far from the hospital, where we spent the night. I wanted to snuggle close to Mother, like Cathie, but I knew better. "I can't be bothered," she would tell me, as she had done so many times before. So I slept on the floor that night.

The next day we drove on to Battle Ground, Washington, to Grandpa and Grandma's house. After a short visit, Aunt Ruth and Uncle Leslie said they had to hurry back to Oakland. I had been expecting them to drive me back to Oakland with them, but apparently they didn't want to be bothered with me. The excitement of seeing Grandma relieved my sadness, and I waved a cheerful good-bye.

Grandma hugged me and loved me, though I could not remember ever having seen her before. My grandparents had a one-story house with a large, unheated, unfinished attic. We lived in that attic for nine months. The house had no indoor plumbing, only a "little house" out back. The thought of going out to the "little house" alone after dark terrified me, so Grandma gave us a "slop jar" to put under the bed to use at night. We all did. A long, narrow flight of stairs led down to the main part of the house. I felt pleased that nobody trusted me to take the slop jar and empty it in the little house each morning.

My great-grandfather also lived with Grandpa and Grandma. He was a Dutchman from Amsterdam and always had time to take me on his lap, tell me stories, and play his violin for me. No one had ever given me this kind of attention before! Most of his stories came from Holland, where his father had been a physician and in the wintertime would skate on the canals to make house calls. Great-grandfather made me feel loved.

He and my grandparents lived in the village of Meadow Glade, which had quite a few houses, a church, a Christian school, a store, and barns and livestock. Grandma would talk to me about Jesus and His love for me, pray with me, and make sure I went to church each week. My brother and sister went too, and sometimes Mother, but she often complained that she wasn't well enough to go to church.

As she began feeling better after the accident, however, she grew restless. It was time to move back to California, she told us. I knew I would miss Grandma and the aunts and uncles, but I was excited because I thought I might get to see Aunt Ruth and Uncle Leslie again. Not many days later Mother bought us bus tickets to California and mentioned that I would again be taking care of Al while Cathie was in school.

Even though I was just a little girl, I had learned to love and trust Jesus. "Give thanks to the Lord Almighty, for the Lord is good; His love endures forever" Jeremiah 33:11 *NIV*.

Chapter 2

The Authorities

*M*other rented a room in a house in Oakland for $15 a month, the same amount Daddy paid for child support, and found a job at The Penny-a-dish Cafeteria. There she received her pay in the form of leftover food, and she would come home each day with a shopping bag full of food for the three of us. We would peek out the window, watching with eager anticipation, until we saw her coming down the sidewalk with the bag. We had no refrigeration, so we ate all we wanted for supper, leaving food that wouldn't quickly spoil for the next morning.

While Mother worked, Cathie went to school, and I took care of my little brother. I was four and a half years old and felt very responsible. Mother ordered me to keep the door to the room locked and never open it for anyone, for if the "authorities" found out that she was leaving us alone, she would get in trouble.

She usually locked Al and me in the closet when she left. Oh, how I hated the closet, because it was dark and cramped and had no place to go to the bathroom. Sometimes Al and I would whisper to each other until we fell asleep. I didn't dare sing, because someone might hear me and report us to the authorities. But I did start talking often to Jesus in the closet. He became my Best Friend.

As a little boy, almost three, Al let me know that he didn't always like my "mothering," but wouldn't cry or yell if I mentioned the authorities. Mother left the key to the closet lying on the table so my sister could let us out to go to the bathroom when she got home from school.

After a few months, Mother found a job with the State Relief Association and she rented a house closer to work. I liked living there, especially because of the fenced backyard. It was large and full of weeds and dirt to use in making roads for our pretend cars—cars we made out of pieces of wood we scavenged. Some people from the church gave us some furniture, and at Christmas, when they gave us a box of food, there was a doll inside for me, made out of a man's sock.

1933

One day when the mailman came to the porch, he rang the doorbell, and though Mother had told me not to open the door for anyone, I felt safe, since this was the mailman. I opened the door a little way, and he squatted down in front of me, unzipped his pants, and exposed himself. I was frightened and couldn't remember ever before having seen a man with his trousers unzipped and open before. I jumped back and slammed the door, grabbed Al, and we dove under the bed where we felt safer and asked Jesus to take care of us.

The time passed slowly until Mother came home. When I told her what had happened, she walked down to the pay phone at the store and called Aunt Ruth and Uncle Leslie, asking them if she could borrow their police dog for a few months to stay with us until she could make other arrangements.

Uncle Leslie brought Rentie over that evening, but the landlord didn't want the dog in the house, so Mother came up with a different plan. She told me to take Al and go into the backyard each day before the mailman arrived. I remember peering through the cracks in the old wooden fence, watching for the mailman. Then, after he would leave, Al and I would go back inside the house. Mother assured me that our guardian angels were taking care of us. I prayed a lot and wanted to believe her, but at age five I was terribly frightened.

Weeks and months passed, and Aunt Ruth and Uncle Leslie no longer talked to me about going to live with them. I began to understand that they weren't going to adopt me after all. I asked

Mother about it, and she told me to mind my own business. I was disappointed but knew I couldn't say anymore. I assumed they didn't want me after all and I wondered why, but I did know that Mother needed me to take care of Al, so I decided to do the best job I could and trust in Jesus to take care of me.

Mother found another house for us to rent, closer to her work. Uncle Leslie helped us move our few belongings and we settled in East Oakland. The house was old and needed painting, and the floorboards on the porch were worn through. There was no landscaping, but at least the roof didn't leak, and it had indoor plumbing.

A kind, white-haired lady lived across the street, and she said I could call her Ma Holt. She had lots of pretty roses; I especially liked the pink ones. She also raised many bright-yellow marigolds and nasturtiums. She let me help pick off the dead flowers sometimes and do some weeding, but she never invited me into her house. I could only imagine how cozy her home must be.

The Long family lived next door. They had a daughter, Mary Belle, about my age and a son, Eugene, about Al's age. Mrs. Long talked gently to me and mentioned that her husband had noticed that my face twitched a lot and that I couldn't see very well. But when she spoke to Mother about it, Mother said she could do nothing about it, because she didn't have enough money. But Mrs. Long went ahead and made an appointment with their eye doctor anyway, and when the day of my appointment came, the Longs took me in their car and paid for the examination and the glasses. I felt so very special! I was six years old and so thankful to them for caring so much. I thanked Jesus for such kind neighbors.

1935

One day I woke up feeling sick and feverish, with a hot, red rash covering my body. Scarlet fever was ravaging the area at that time, and when the neighbors heard I was sick, they reported me to the authorities. A doctor came to see me and confirmed that I had scarlet fever and told Mother that we would be quarantined. So the authorities placed a "Quarantined" sign on the front of our house, meaning that no one could leave or come in until further notice. This made Mother very angry. In harsh tones she asked us children how she was supposed to support us if she couldn't work. She told me it was my fault and that if it were not for me, she wouldn't be in this mess. I was hot and itchy and didn't feel good at all, but Mother's words and tone of voice made me feel even worse. All I could do was talk to Jesus and ask Him to make me well. At least Mother was there to take care of Brother Al.

Finally, after they determined that I was no longer contagious, the authorities took the sign down, but insisted on fumigating the house. So we moved our beds out into the shed and stayed there while the house was being disinfected. When we were able to move back in, it seemed so good to get things back to normal, so Mother could go back to work.

A little later we all got the flu at the same time, and someone called an ambulance to take us all to the county hospital. Because there was a flu epidemic, the hospital had crowded the beds close together and even out into the halls. There were no private rooms. They sent Al to the kids' ward, but he was so afraid he cried loudly. So the nurses finally brought him back to the ward where I was and put his crib by my bed. I prayed with him and talked to him and finally got him quieted down, to everyone's relief.

Mother and Cathie were ready for discharge first, but the doctor said that Al and I weren't well enough to leave. I didn't like it one bit, so I talked to Jesus and asked Him to help us get well fast. Aunt Ruth and Uncle Leslie said we could stay in their attic until we were well enough to go home, so in a couple days they discharged Al and me, and Uncle Leslie took us to his house. Rentie, their dog, jumped for joy when he saw us. I entertained my brother by making paper airplanes and sailing them out the window. We had a lot of fun, until I got in trouble for messing up the yard.

When we moved back to our little house, Mother decided we should start going to church. I jumped up and down in eager anticipation. At church, a kind teenager named Margaret took a liking to me and met me each week. I loved it when she asked me to sit with her. I enjoyed the little papers they gave us at church each week, and sometimes Mother read us stories from them.

Mr. Albright, an elderly newspaper salesman with only one arm, lived a couple houses up the street. He told Mother that if she would prepare a warm meal for him each evening, he would give her enough food so we could have a warm meal too. This worked out very well for quite awhile. Mother would have my sister carry the food to his house; sometimes she would send me along to carry a non-breakable dish (she felt I was clumsy and could not be trusted with breakable dishes.) She claimed she had never seen another kid as clumsy as me. I tried to be careful, but I was always hurrying, thinking: *"If I could do everything better, or faster, maybe Mother would approve. Maybe next time!"*

One day when Al and I were home alone, I got the idea of building a playhouse. We had an old wooden fence in the backyard, about six feet tall, with rusty nails sticking out here and there, and I figured I could nail some boards across the top of the fence to form a roof. I wasn't quite tall enough, so I rolled an old stump up beside the fence, climbed onto it, and set about pulling out some of the old nails I planned to straighten and reuse. But when the stump wobbled, I fell to the ground.

I could tell by the pain that my right leg above my knee was badly injured, and when I checked it out, I saw a wide-open, three-inch gash. Shocked, I began screaming and running for Ma Holt's house, with Al following me and yelling for all he was worth. The woman who lived next to Ma Holt's house heard us and called us to her house, took us inside, and pulled the wound together with a big piece of adhesive tape. She then asked me where she could find our Mother.

We told her she had gone to visit "Aunt Ruth," but it took me awhile to remember Aunt Ruth's last name. When we finally located her number in the phone book, she called Mother. Mother had to walk three miles home, and when she arrived, she asked Mr. Albright if he would take us to the doctor. He seemed happy to help.

We went to see Dr. Miller, who had once adjusted Mother's back. Mother held down my leg as the doctor tore off the tape, put in three stitches, and then bandaged it up again (it would leave an ugly scar). All the while Mother was telling me how clumsy I was and how she didn't know how she could ever pay the doctor's bill. I felt terrible to have caused Mother so much trouble. *Maybe next time I could be more careful.* I asked Jesus to help me.

Mother was working part time for the school system and did odd jobs, washing and ironing to make a little extra money. She knew that the state disapproved of her leaving us children alone, so she told us, "Now, you make sure you don't let anyone in."

She held up a passkey and showed us how to put it in the lock and turn it to the side, so no one could put in a key from the other side. She made my sister and me practice until we got it right. It scared me, because I didn't want the "authorities" to find out we were there alone, so I talked often to my Friend Jesus about our situation.

Then it happened. Al and I were alone when I heard someone come up the front steps. I knew I had put the key in and turned it in both locks, so I grabbed my little brother, pushed him under the bed, and crawled in beside him, whispering that we needed to be very quiet. Then I prayed to Jesus.

The visitor knocked, then put a key in the door. Those old-fashioned skeleton keys were different than keys made today, and anyone who had a skeleton key could unlock any other house that used a similar lock—unless something was blocking the keyhole. I was praying that Jesus would protect us and keep mother from getting in trouble.

Then the footsteps went down the front steps and around the house to the back and up the back steps, stopping as someone put a key in the door. I complimented myself for putting our key in the right way.

But still my heart was pounding. I thanked Jesus for helping us and whispered to my brother to be very quiet. As I heard the footsteps fading away, I crawled out from under the bed and very quietly went to the front window and pulled the dark shade away just a crack. I could see a lady getting into her car and driving away. I let out a long breath, pulled my little brother to me and knelt on the floor under the window and thanked Jesus for taking care of us.

When Mother came home, I told her about it. She said, "Well, you did the right thing." I was thrilled to hear Mother's words of approval.

Uncle Leslie did landscaping for a business and had no place to dispose of limbs and branches, and Mother said he could leave them in our backyard, and she would burn them. One day when she set out to burn the pile, a little breeze came up, and the fire started to work its way through the dead grass in the backyard.

Mother quickly sent my sister to a corner fire alarm, about two blocks away. All my sister had to do was to break the glass, pull down the black lever, wait for the fire engine to show up, and direct them to our house. In the meantime Mother shouted to me to get my little brother out of the way. I grabbed him and made a beeline for the house, and yes, straight for the bed. We slithered under it and I prayed, "Dear Jesus, please help the house not to burn down, and please help Mother not to get into trouble with the authorities." Pretty soon we heard the fire engine arrive and men shouting and water running. We shook and prayed until it became quiet outside. When we ventured out from under the bed, I didn't have the courage to go outside, but peeked out the back window. I saw that the blackened grass came almost all the way up to the house. Jesus had answered my prayers once again.

One day I was feeling very alone. I had learned to play a little bit by ear on an old piano that someone had given us. I started to play and sing a song that I had heard at church, "It Was Alone the Savior

Prayed, in Dark Gethsemane." Mother came up and hit me in the side of the head, and in her most angry voice said, "Don't you ever let me hear you play or sing that song again!" I was absolutely crushed! I thought *if she had just taken me in her arms and asked me why I sang that song. If she had just told me that she loved me.* But no, she hit me again and told me to get out. *Maybe later!*

Mother had a hard life and probably did the best she knew how, but she was angry a lot. When her frustrations got out of hand, she took them out by hitting and kicking me. Cathie was a comfort to her, kind of a confidante. Mother's life would have been much happier without me. Why she felt that way she never told me, and I tried so hard to be good.

My sister didn't really know what to do about Mother hitting me so much, but she was flattered that Mother confided in her, and she rarely encouraged me or showed sympathy. My brother loved me, though he sometimes acted as little brothers do. But he loved me and respected me, and still does.

1936

The authorities contacted Mother and told her that since I would soon be eight, by law I had to go to school. What would she do now with my little brother, since he wasn't quite old enough for school? She contacted her parents, who said they would take care of him for a while, in Washington. Going to school made me happy, but how I missed Al!

Mother enrolled Cathie and me in Golden Gate Academy, a Christian 12-grade school, and a kind woman in our church volunteered to pay my tuition that first year—$3 per month. I was grateful. Aunt Ruth had helped me learn to read already, and I had a quick mind and enjoyed being around other kids. But the school was a long way from where we lived, which meant riding the streetcar for about an hour each way and finding a way to pay the bus fare.

By February my sister and I were both exhausted and sickly, and Mother decided to send us to the public school, just two miles away. She told the principal that I wasn't well, so every afternoon the teacher made me lie down on my blanket and take a nap. I didn't like it very much, but I usually went to sleep.

Being taller and older than anyone else in the first grade, I felt out of place. My teacher was kind and asked if I would like to take some tests to see if I could qualify to move up to the second grade. I agreed and passed with flying colors. I didn't feel so awkward in the second grade, and I quickly learned that if I did all my work on time and was nice to everyone, my teacher would be pleased with me. I began to think that maybe the authorities weren't so bad after all.

"Remind the people to be subject to rulers and authorities, to be obedient, to be ready to do whatever is good, to slander no one, to be peaceable and considerate, and to show true humility toward all men" Titus 3:1 *NIV*.

Roen, Cathie, Al, circa 1935

Four generations Front row: Cathie, Roen, Al Back row: Bernice, Sophia (Bernice's mother), Olive, (Sophia's mother), circa 1936

The Wilsons: front row, Shirley, Sheila. Back row: Charles Marion, Zelia, Everett, Roen

Everett on his first day of school in 1933

Roen, 8th grade graduation 1942

Roen and Terry

Roen, Cathie, and Cathie Lee, at McLaughlin Heights

Chapter 3

My Commitment

We moved to Berkeley, California, that summer, about three blocks from Golden Gate Academy, where Mother had enrolled Cathie and me. She'd decided to leave Al with her parents for a while. No more naps, and it just took a few minutes to get to school. I was happy. Mother's sister, Emma, and her brother, Ducas, from Washington, surprised us with a visit. They told Mother they planned to live in St. Helena, California, and offered to take me with them. Mother seemed very happy about such an arrangement. I had been getting acquainted with my classmates and didn't want to make another change, but if it would be better for Mother, I would go.

1938

Uncle Ducas took me to a little one-room Christian school in St. Helena, California, with only one teacher. She seemed very nice, but I wondered how things would go. Her nicely kept white hair framed her kind face, and I noticed that her right arm was missing. A wood stove heated the room. Each morning she sent several of us outside to the large woodpile to bring in enough wood for the day. It made me happy to be able to help her.

She explained to my uncle, "This is an eight-grade school, and we have had no third-graders this year." But after examining my report card and noting my age, she asked my uncle if he would allow me to go into the fourth grade, if I tested well. He agreed. So I went into the fourth grade. I was happy; now I was in the same grade as my peers. Time passed quickly. Before I realized it, school was out, and Uncle Ducas and Aunt Emma decided we should move back to Washington. It was good to see Grandma again, but we didn't stay long before they told me that my mother wanted me back in California. I thought, *"Oh, good, maybe my mother wants to see me!"*

Aunt Emma's boyfriend, Ken, said that he and a friend were going to California and could take me home. So I got into the car with those two men, whom I didn't know at all, and we headed down the coastal route. (I'd packed my few clothes in a paper bag, since I didn't have a suitcase.) I thought they drove very fast, and they stopped only once to get something to eat at a restaurant. They invited me to go in with them, but I said, "No, thank you, I will just wait in the car." I didn't have any money, and I didn't want to ask them to feed me. When they came back to the car they brought me a candy bar. It looked mighty good to me, because I didn't get to have candy bars very often.

In time I became very uncomfortable because I needed to go to the bathroom, but I refused to say a word and just held it. Years later Uncle Ken told me about this trip and said he couldn't figure out what was wrong with me, why I didn't even get out of the car and go to the bathroom.

When we arrived Mother didn't act very glad to see me. She told me to take my paper bag into the house and she would be in later. I didn't understand. Why had she said I had to come home? I vowed to try my best to make her happy, and I asked my Friend Jesus to help me.

I was at home alone a lot and I wanted someone to love me and talk to. I worked cleaning the school after classes were out, then went home to do the chores there that Mother and Cathie had assigned me. We didn't have a radio, but I liked to read, so I spent a lot of time in the world of "Pollyanna" and other old-time favorites.

Our next-door neighbors had a daughter named Dorothy, who did not go to my school. Mother mentioned to Dorothy's mother that I really needed to have my tonsils out, and that they were having a tonsil clinic at the school, and anyone could get their tonsils out for $5, but that she didn't have the money. Dorothy's mother said, "Dorothy needs her tonsils out too. Do you think they would take Dorothy's tonsils out for five dollars if we paid for Roen's surgery too?" Mother talked to the "Tonsil Clinic" people, and they said that would be fine.

Clinic day arrived, and the gymnasium and chapel floors were filled with cots and blankets. I rode to the school with Dorothy and her parents. Most of the kids had their mother or father with them, and I wished Mother had come with me, but she said she didn't have time. I was taken into a little room and a mask was put over my face, and a nurse began to drop ether onto it. I wanted to scream. I didn't like that thing on my face. Soon I began to feel drowsy, and the next thing I knew, I was on one of the cots and my throat hurt a whole lot. I wanted to cry, but I knew that if anyone told Mother that I'd cried, she would be really mad at me, so I just lay there and waited and talked to my Friend Jesus.

1939

We started going to church in Berkeley, about three miles away, and of course we walked to the services. Often Mother would say she didn't feel well and would tell Cathie and me to go ahead. The pastor held some baptismal classes at the church for those who wanted to make a commitment to Jesus. I took the classes and learned so much.

The day I was baptized was special for the members, because it was the first service in their new church. As we prepared for the baptism, a lady asked me to take off my dress and gave me a dark robe, which I slipped over my head. I felt strange in it, but I did what they asked me to do. Then the deaconess helped me walk out to the baptistery and I stood in line with the others. When my turn came, Pastor Taylor baptized me. I felt pleased to be a new Christian!

A few people at church shook my hand, gave me hugs, and congratulated me on my decision. Mother had not attended, saying she didn't feel well, so when I got home after church Mother said, "See if you can find something to eat." That was the extent of my baptismal celebration in our home.

The new Berkeley church was beautiful. When the sun shown through the stained glass windows, it cast a warm, rosy glow. A big picture of Jesus graced the front wall, and green plants surrounded the baptismal font.

We never invited anyone home for dinner because we didn't have enough food. In fact, one day, when I attended church alone, I invited a girlfriend over for dinner. She complained about the long walk to my house, and when we finally got there, the only thing I could find in the way of food was a can of spinach, which I opened and offered to her. She frowned and said she wanted to go home. I never invited anyone over again from church, and no one ever invited us over for dinner, either.

Our church had prayer meeting every Wednesday night, and I thought, *"I'm a new Christian, and I need to go to prayer meeting,"* so on Wednesday nights I'd walk the three miles to prayer meeting by myself. I often didn't feel safe.

World War II was in full swing, and as I stood at the front door of the church one evening, looking over the city with its shining lights, all of a sudden the air raid siren began to wail, and all the lights went out! It was the strangest feeling to look out over Berkeley and see nothing but darkness. It made me feel dizzy; overwhelmed with fear. I thought we were going to be bombed. All of the lights had been turned off inside the church, too, and the deacons were rounding everybody up, asking them to sit in the middle section of the church to avoid any falling glass. We sat there singing, "Under His wings, I am safely abiding." It was a fearsome moment—a time of learning to trust, to talk to God, and ask for His care and protection.

The pastor spoke about how much God loves us and that He would protect us, as He saw fit. When the all clear sounded we rejoiced together. The lights came back on, but we still had no idea why the sirens had gone off. That evening after the service, as I walked alone in the dark, fear continued to grip me. I was afraid that whatever had caused the sirens to sound in the first place might still be lurking in the dark. I talked to Jesus the whole way home— *He must have been busy that night!*

The government had a plan for distributing surplus food to the poor. Farms, orchards, and grocery companies that had outdated, or extra, food donated it to the program. Sometimes there would be grapefruit, oranges, and prunes. I can remember sitting on the curb, eating an orange, and relishing every bite, feeling so blessed. I really didn't know we were poor. My mother often said that we couldn't afford this or that, but I thought everybody lived as we did.

Mother worked for "Works Progress Administration," usually referred to as *WPA*. It was a public program designed by President Franklin D. Roosevelt to help people recover financially after the Great Depression. Mother worked in Berkeley. She walked the three miles each way to work, until one day Daddy brought my sister a bicycle for her birthday. After that Mother rode the bicycle to work and that made her life easier. She would ride the bike home in the evening, have a bite to eat, then take the streetcar to night school at Merritt Business College. She got a high school diploma there and was determined to get more education and better our situation.

Cathie, who was four and a half years older than I, had her own friends. She and Mother talked together a lot, but Cathie didn't have much to say to me. I felt like an outcast. When Mother asked Cathie to do a lot of work, Cathie in turn made me do a lot of it, and I didn't like that. I was always willing to work hard, but I didn't like people taking advantage of me. For example, when she washed the dishes, she always made me do the kettles. I resented that!

One day I found a dime in the gutter and pondered long about what I could do with it. I knew that Mother loved U-No bars, but rarely ever had one. At the Safeway store you could buy three for a dime, and they were bigger than they are now. I bought three and gave them to my mother. She gave me a bite of one. I felt so happy. Maybe I could win *her approval*.

1939

Daddy would occasionally take Al and Cathie to a park to play, or out for a soda or ice cream cone, but he'd never take me with them. I had no idea at that time why. It just hurt. I tried to talk to Mother about it, but she would become very angry and tell me to shut up. He brought my sister gifts—like a clock or a typewriter—but there was never anything for me.

During one of Daddy's visits, I heard him tell Al and Cathie that he had now married a fine, Christian woman. She had nine children, but only four were still at home. Her name was Belle. When my sister asked what they should call her, Daddy said that they should refer to her by whatever made them feel comfortable. But Daddy didn't include me in the conversations, and there were no hugs.

The next Christmas, when I was 10 years old, Daddy came with some gifts for the other kids, and a brown bag for me. I peeked inside, and there was a pretty celluloid dresser set—comb, brush, and mirror. I was ecstatic. He apologized that it wasn't wrapped in pretty paper. But it was my first gift ever—from either Mother or Daddy. From then on, whenever he came to see my brother and sister, he included me; it brought such joy to my young heart. I was glad Daddy had remarried.

I started the fifth grade that fall, back at Golden Gate Academy. Since I had been there only off and on, I didn't know any of my classmates. I earned my expenses by cleaning classrooms after school and during the summer. Things always needed to be scrubbed or painted, and I worked enough to pay all my tuition. The teachers all knew me because I worked so much, and they liked me because I never complained. I was getting appreciation, and I loved it! In my heart I thought, *"Oh, I really like this!"* I was now almost 12 years old.

1941

My brother Al was now back at home, and we were always hungry. I didn't know it until years later, when he told me, that he would go to the grocery store where they displayed fruit out front, walk along the sidewalk, pick up an apple or an orange, and go around the corner and eat it. He said he got caught just once, but that he had stolen a lot of fruit because he felt so hungry. The next time Mother went in to pay our bill, the grocer angrily told her that he never wanted to see Al at his store again, and that she could no longer charge food there.

Mother cried, scolded, and spanked Al. She contacted her sister Gertie, in Washington, and it was agreed that Al would go to Washington to live with Gertie and her family for a while.

Doing the laundry took a lot of my time. We didn't have a washing machine anymore, just a washboard and a big tub that I filled with water for rinsing. I'd rub the clothes hard on the washboard and wring them out by hand, forming huge blisters between my thumbs and my index fingers from twisting the sheets. Not knowing any better, I just kept scrubbing and wringing the clothes until the blisters popped. How they hurt! When Mother came home I showed her my blisters, but she just yelled, "You should know better! You have to wring the clothes easier. Maybe this will teach you!"

Our church had an activity they called Ingathering. A group of us would walk along the sidewalk and sing favorite gospel songs, while a few others rang doorbells and requested donations for the poor. One of the young men reached over once and held my hand as we were walking along. I didn't know anything about holding hands, and when I got home I told Cathie about it and mentioned his name. To my horror, she sat down on the floor and started to cry. I thought to myself, *"I don't even like him, and here she is upset because she wants him."* She wouldn't talk to me anymore, and I had no idea how to handle the situation. *What was I supposed to do when he took my hand and held it? Was I supposed to jerk it away, or act like I liked it, or what? Who could I ask?*

My sister's new boyfriend, Dick, was in the Navy. She had met him at the roller rink. Joe, a young man in our church, had taken an interest in me, and his parents had a car they occasionally would let him use. One Saturday night Dick asked Joe if the four of us could go to China Town in San Francisco in his car. Joe agreed. We spent a little time looking around, and then it was time to start for home. Dick volunteered to drive us back. Joe agreed.

Pretty soon I felt Joe slip his arm around me and kind of hug me up to him. I had no idea what I was supposed to do! Should I act completely relaxed and let him draw me to him, or should I hug back? I hadn't been hugged before by anyone except my Grandma. But I figured it out eventually, and rather liked it.

One day a man showed up at our house and said that the principal at the Christian school had told him that mother might be able to furnish room and board for his daughter, who would be a junior in high school that year. The man, Ervin, was in the middle of a divorce—his wife had left him for his brother. Mother decided that it would be a good idea to take the girl, as it would help her pay our rent. So she turned the living room into a bedroom. My sister and Louise, the new girl, each had a twin bed to sleep on, and I had a little cot. There wouldn't have been room for another regular bed.

Ervin and Mother shared their woes and soon fell in love. He lived about 50 miles away but would frequently come on one of the weekend days and take Mother for a drive so they could get better acquainted.

1942

While I was in the eighth grade, our teacher became sick, and we had one substitute after another. Some of the kids were acting up, and I mentioned it to Mother. She said that she would write to her brother, Andy, who lived at Battle Ground, Washington, and see if I could finish the school year up there. Al was already living in Washington, with Mother's sister, Gertie, and Cathie and Louise were at Walla Walla, Washington, living with Grandma and Grandpa.

Uncle Andy said that I could come stay with them and finish out the eighth grade, so she sent me on the Dollar Lines Bus. After I left, Mother had a lot more time to spend on her courtship.

I knew Uncle Andy and Aunt Tomie a little bit from when I had been in the fourth grade. They had a baby girl and lived in a tiny house beside a large shop where Uncle Andy made his living doing mechanical work on cars. There was an unfinished attic, without insulation, over the garage that they used mostly for storage. They pushed their things to one side and put a bed up there for me. Aunt Tomie and Uncle Andy were good to me, and I appreciated their kindness.

Most of the time I walked the four miles each way to and from school—two miles on highway, two on gravel. Eventually they were able to arrange for me to ride the public school bus for three of those miles, a welcome change, but anytime I wanted to go to a school function, I had to walk. I was a lonely teenager, in a new school. I didn't quite know how to handle it.

One Saturday night after a program at the school, I started out for home. I had only gone a short way when a car pulled up beside me, and Clarence Wade, one of the boys from the school, said, "Jump in, we will take you home." There were several other young people in the car that I knew, so I agreed to go with them. Clarence said, "Why don't you take off your coat?" He was sitting awfully close to me. Being 13 and very naïve, I said, "What for, I'm a bit chilly." Clarence told the driver, "We had better take Roen home; I know her uncle and he won't want her to be out late."

Eighth-grade graduation was a big event for me. Aunt Tomie and Uncle Andy had only said I could stay until I finished school that year. But Mother was enjoying courting and working and didn't know what to do with me. My sister, Cathie, had just graduated from high school and now had a job and her own apartment. She convinced Mother that she would help with my expenses if Mother would let me go back to California. I found a ride with friends and looked forward to life back in Berkeley.

I enrolled at Golden Gate Academy. Mother rented two rooms in the upstairs of a home near the academy, and we put our beds in one room and stored the rest of our belongings in the other. We had no kitchen facilities, so we just lunched. That meant no warm food, no refrigeration, and no dishes to wash.

I got a job in the principal's office, keeping track of attendance for the students. I had a desk just inside the front door in the main hall. It felt good to be trusted and appreciated. I took typing and it came very easily for me. Soon I was typing letters and answering the phone along with other duties in the principal's office.

Mother had taught me to sew several years before when I wanted a skirt with many seams in it. When I finished it I proudly showed it to her expecting words of approval. Instead she screamed at me, "You made the seams too narrow. They will pull out. You have to pull out all that stitching and do it right." I'd been crushed but determined, and carefully did as I was told. It was a good lesson.

Mrs. Jones, one of the teachers at my school, asked Mother to make some curtains for her house. Mother told her that she didn't have time, but that I would make them. I did, and when they were finished, I carefully pressed and folded them. Mrs. Jones told me I had done a beautiful job and that she liked them very much.

As I visited with Mrs. Jones, she commented that since I could already sew so well, I probably would not need to take sewing at school. She said she would talk to the sewing teacher about it. It got me thinking: *If I didn't have to take sewing and still got credit for it, maybe by adding another class each year and taking one in the summer, I could graduate in three years. It would save a lot of money, and I could be out on my own, earning money sooner.*

When I spoke with the sewing teacher, she mentioned hearing that I was a good seamstress and that if I wanted to challenge the course, I could do so by taking a test and making three garments— an apron, a blouse, and a makeover. No problem. I went to work on the projects, finished them quickly, took the test, and got an "A" in sewing.

Church was a bright spot in my life, and I always tried to participate in youth activities. Each winter a group of us would go Ingathering for several nights, and I enjoyed being with others and singing. One night a young man named John asked if I would like to ride with him. Later, as we walked along, singing the old gospel hymns, his hand lightly brushed mine. I felt a mixture of a shock and a chill! My voice wavered, and I flushed as I looked up at him. He took my hand and gave it a reassuring squeeze. We began singing, "In the Garden," and when we came to the chorus, "And He walks with me and He talks with me, and He tells me I am His own," John tenderly squeezed my hand again. Oh, it was so hard to remember to sing clearly and focus on the needy for whom we were providing.

When we returned to the church, John said, "May I give you a ride home?" I'd always walked to and from church, though now his offer sounded tempting; but what would people say? Finally I decided that it would be all right, just this once.

That evening I bounced into the house, straight into the inquiring gaze of my sister; "How did you get home so early, did they quit singing so soon?" I wondered if I should share anything about this wonderful, new feeling yet, or if I should just savor it in my heart for a while. Casually I said, "Oh, I got a ride home."

"A ride home!" Cathie exclaimed, "And who, may I ask, gave you a ride home?"

I answered that it was John, and it that was so nice not to have to make that long walk alone in the dark.

"John!" she exploded. "Do you know how old he is? He's five years older than you are! Nita and I have noticed how he's been paying attention to you. We think it's scandalous. He should be paying attention to one of us older girls!"

"Oh no," I said quietly, "Do you really think it is wrong for me to let him bring me home?"

"Well, it would certainly be better if you would stick to someone your own age, if you want to have a boyfriend!" Cathie shouted.

As I plowed into the pile of dirty dishes, my thoughts raced back and forth from joy—great, unfamiliar joy!—to old, familiar sadness. I wanted so much to do what was right, to win approval, to "be good." Was it bad that my spine tingled and that I could almost burst with joy when John looked at me with sparkling eyes of understanding and acceptance? Oh, if only I had someone to talk to, someone who would understand, someone who knew right from wrong. Was it scandalous? Why did my sister say this? I was trying to do what was right. Wasn't it all right to feel such happiness?

As I said my prayers that evening, I thanked God for this new happiness, and asked Him to help me understand. I would do what was right. God was my Best Friend, and I wouldn't let Him down. I would not be involved in anything scandalous!

I walked to church as usual on the very next Ingathering night. Sure enough, there was John with a broad, caring smile. I knew I must be careful. I must do the right thing. I decided that I would let him hold my hand as we walked along and sang, but of course, I wouldn't let him take me home. We had a fun, blissful time, until he asked if I would like a ride home. I couldn't bring myself to tell him that it was scandalous for me to let him pay attention to me, so I simply said, "Thank you very much, but I would rather walk."

Oh dear, now I had told a lie, but maybe that was better than everyone knowing that I was letting an "older man" pay attention to me. As I walked away from the church, I looked back and saw him standing there, watching me. I wanted to run back and tell him that

I had changed my mind; that I would love to have a ride home. But no, I had to do what was right!

World War II raged on, and all available young men were being drafted into the service. Dick had proposed to my sister, Cathie, and they were soon to be married. I was busy with my studies and work at school and was surprised by a knock on the door one evening. There stood John. He told me that he had come to tell me good-bye. He had received his greetings from Uncle Sam and would be leaving in two days. The news made me sad. After he left that evening, I called some friends to see if they could help me have a party for him. They said sure, we could have it at their house. So I got to see him once again.

From time to time I would see his parents at church and ask what they heard from him. They never gave me much information, so I thought probably the story was true, about his being interested in a girl who lived in the Northwest.

I couldn't blame him, after the way I turned down his offers to take me home. *Maybe next time!*

The Bible classes at the Christian school increased my knowledge and reinforced the commitment I had made to God; they also fortified my resolve to do the right thing.

I was determined to study and learn all I could from the Bible. I took these words to heart, *"Do your best to present yourself to God as one approved, a workman who does not need to be ashamed and who correctly handles the word of truth"* 2 Timothy 2:15 *NIV.*

Chapter 4

On the Move Again

1943

*M*y mother and her new fiancé moved to Washington, where she stayed with her parents and he lived with some of his relatives. Since they planned to be married soon, they rented a rundown, one-room house. As soon as school was out, Mother told me that they had decided to move to Washington for good and for me to bring as many of her things with me up from California as I could manage on the bus. Since my sister was soon to be married, I would no longer have a place to live with relatives in California.

I packed many of Mother's household items—iron, waffle iron, kitchen utensils, dishes, and towels—into her old, copper wash boiler and tied the lid on securely. It was so heavy I could barely lift it. I packed some other things in boxes and tied them up, making several trips on the streetcar to get everything down to the bus depot. The wash boiler, of course, posed serious problems getting on and off the streetcar, but somehow I managed.

I had a ticket to take a Dollar Lines bus, which always carried its luggage on top. When the driver hefted the heavy wash boiler, at first he refused to take it. But when I pled with him and told him my mother would be very angry if I didn't take it, he finally relented.

When I arrived at the Portland depot where Mother was supposed to meet me, no one showed up. I was distraught. What should I do with my pile of stuff? Finally I saw Ervin's son walking toward me. He assured me that he was supposed to meet me and transport the things I had brought and that Mother and Ervin would see me in Battle Ground. In about an hour we arrived home to a structure that resembled a shack, with no inside plumbing and no place for me to sleep. The floor would be my bed the first night.

Mother and Ervin were married at the Justice of the Peace, but we kids weren't invited. I have no idea who served as their witnesses. The next day Ervin hitched up his team of horses to the logging that was better than nothing, and I worked each day until Al's school got out at 3:30. It made for long days, and finally the folks decided to let us ride our horse Queenie bareback, to and from school. This presented some problems, since I didn't like the idea of smelling like a horse all day at school. I also found it difficult to modestly get up on the horse while wearing a skirt, but Ervin forbade me to wear any kind of pants, since in his view it was a sin for women to dress like men.

Somehow, though, I got hold of an old pair of pants, and Al would stop the horse down the road, out of sight of the house, and I would pull those old pants on up under my skirt. Then I would get back on the horse, and carefully hold my skirt up so that it wouldn't touch Queenie. When we were almost to the school, Al would again stop the horse, and I would jump off, pull down the pants, put them in a bag, and walk the remaining block or two to school. I wouldn't dare let anybody see me with those old pants hanging down under my dress. Al would always take Queenie to the pasture where we had arranged for her to stay during the day.

Mother was able to find a job at the public library in Vancouver, Washington, and carpooled with a neighbor who worked at the same place and would pick her up and drop her off at our house. This helped considerably, but money was still very tight.

One day as Al and I started out for school, we looked back toward our home and saw smoke coming out of the roof, around the chimney edges. Al started running and screaming that the house was on fire. Soon neighbors responded and said they had called the fire department. The firefighters arrived shortly and were able to put out the roof fire, where sparks from the chimney had ignited the room.

To avoid a recurrence, they laid a large, metal sheet around the chimney to protect the roof, and Ervin repaired the damage and we assumed everything was good.

But a week or so later, as we were eating breakfast, we heard a car racing toward the house with its horn honking. We opened the door and heard someone scream, "Fire, fire." We ran outside, grabbing a few things as we went. The neighbors again had called the fire department, and the firemen were able to put the fire out before everything was destroyed. But this time the fire had burned a lot of the roof and the fire department gave us notice that the house was not habitable—that we could no longer live in it.

Ervin, an experienced carpenter and builder, asked the owner of the property if he would provide the money for materials to build a one-room cottage on the property. The owner agreed to this arrangement.

Still we had no plumbing, but it gave Ervin and Mother a place to sleep. For Al and me he bought two old army tents for $5 each, and we put them up and moved in. We still had the old springs that we'd salvaged from the scrap metal place, and we laid these on the ground. But when it rained the blankets got wet and we got cold. I soon figured out that when the blankets touched the side of the wet tent, they acted like a wick, and much of the quilt would end up getting wet. It soon smelled moldy, and I began to feel feverish and sick.

Mother's sister Emma came by to see us and was concerned enough about me to offer to take me with her and Uncle Ken to the coast to stay with them for a week or two, until I got to feeling better.

There was no money to pay for a doctor's examination, and antibiotics weren't available yet. But she and Uncle Ken were nice to me, and it helped a lot to be able to sleep in a warm, dry house with indoor plumbing. I thanked Jesus for helping me get better. After about two weeks I was feeling pretty good, and they took me back home to Mother. No hugs, but I buried myself in work and studies. I told my Best Friend how I felt.

When the school had a program or activity that I wanted to attend, I had to walk there alone, since Al wasn't in high school yet and usually did not attend programs at the school. One Saturday night I was walking home alone at about 10:30 p.m., on a long, straight stretch of road. A car passed me, put on the brakes, then made a U-turn, and headed back toward me. Frightened, I dove into the dry ditch beside the road and lay against the ground as flat as I could and waited as the car moved slowly past. Then I scrambled up to where I could see the roadway and saw the car making yet another U-turn. So I hit the bottom of the ditch in a hurry and lay there, praying that Jesus would protect me. The car passed back and forth a half-dozen times. Finally peeking out, I saw the car disappear around a far corner. After a brief chat with my Best Friend Jesus, who I was sure had protected me, I jumped up and ran all the way home. When I got home, I was breathing heavily and went to my tent and to bed, since I was not allowed to go into the cottage and visit with Mother. She and Ervin saw no reason why Al or I should invade their privacy. I prayed that someday things would be different. *Maybe later!*

"With everlasting kindness, I will have compassion on you says the Lord your Redeemer" Isaiah 54:8 *NIV*.

Chapter 5

You're Not Worth Your Salt

*E*rvin bought an old two-wheeled buggy for $10. It had metal wheels and made a lot of noise, but our horse Queenie was willing to pull it. It could carry only two people at a time, and it embarrassed me to ride in it, since no one else rode to church or anywhere else in a buggy anymore.

After church one day, I wanted to stand around and talk to my friends, but Mother came up to me and said, "I will go get the buggy." Pleadingly I said, "Oh no, Mother, I will be right down to help you." Ervin and Al had already started walking home. Next thing I knew, Mother pulled up right in front of the church, and said, "Get in." I had been talking to a young man who I thought was kind of nice, and I was mortified, but I obeyed my mother.

Now Al and I rode to school in the buggy, a huge improvement. We could stay warmer, now, by tucking a quilt around us when it was cold and by pulling the buggy's little cover up over our heads to keep rain and snow off us. This continued my whole junior year, and though at first people would stare at us and laugh, they got used to us after awhile and kind of ignored us. We traveled much slower than the cars, of course, and since the roadway was not wide enough for us to pull over, out of the way of approaching traffic, some motorists became annoyed with us.

The principal at the school called me in one day and said, "You are going to have to do something about your bill. We can't let you go to school here if you don't get your bill paid soon." I told him that I didn't know what to do about it, and that maybe I should just start going to public school. He said, "Oh, we don't want you to do that!" I explained that since I only received 18 cents an hour, there was no way I could pay my bill, and my parents weren't in a position to help me, either.

Mother found out about a janitorial job paying $35 a month at a small public school located a mile from our house. Al and I went to see about the job, and they offered it to us. We knew it was an answer to prayer. But it now meant two more miles a day to either ride or walk. I would now be able do my homework while I waited for Al to get out of school, and then we would go directly to the schoolhouse each day and clean it. We had a lot of incentive to do a good job and to do it quickly. We still went hungry a lot, but during the summer we had a big garden, and I loved it. We also had wild berries on the place, which we canned.

In the fall Mother and Ervin went to California for a week to pick up some of their belongings, while Al and I stayed home to milk the cows. I was 14 and my brother was 12. We both jumped out of bed one morning when the alarm clock sounded to gather in the cows and do the milking. I washed the strainer that I had neglected to wash the night before, and got breakfast. We used a wood cook stove that did double duty by also warming up the kitchen.

This morning, however, it seemed like it was taking Al an extra-long time to milk the nine cows, and I began glancing out the windows, looking for him. I noticed how dark the morning seemed, and that none of the neighbor's lights were on. Finally I checked our clock—it said 2:30! Finally Al came in with a noticeably smaller supply of milk than normal, and it had taken him a lot longer than usual to get the cows to come to the barn for milking. "I don't know, Sis, it's really black out there," he commented.

"Look at the clock!" I replied. By then it said 5 a.m., but we still had a good laugh as we sat down to a good breakfast of oatmeal, toast, and fruit.

While we were eating Grandpa showed up to help us milk. We told him, "Thank you for coming, but they are all milked."

"What?" he replied, taken back.

"Somehow we set the alarm wrong. The milking is all done," we replied.

So we carried the milk in a can and set it by the road for the cheese factory truck to pick up. The can was not nearly as full as usual.

I decided that I didn't want to live in a tent any longer—but what to do? We didn't even have a place to wash dishes in the cottage Ervin had built, and Al and I weren't welcome there, besides. Mother and Ervin had set a table outside the back door where we washed dishes.

One night a young man offered to walk me home after a school program. I didn't really have an eye for him, but I couldn't resist having some company. I told him that it was a long walk, and I didn't have any place for him to come in and rest before starting the long walk back. True to my word, when we got to my tent, I couldn't invite him in or give him a hot drink—anything. I felt bad. The lights were out in the cottage.

No surprise that he never asked to walk me home again. So much for popularity with the young men!

My friend Dena (she and I had been friends since the 8th grade) and I wanted to go away to boarding school for our senior year. I reasoned that if I went at the beginning of the summer, I could work enough to get a good start. It would be wonderful to have a clean, dry bed and a place to shower. I told Mother about our plan and she said it was a good idea but that they would not be able to help me with the expenses.

Columbia Academy, the school we had been attending, had hired a new principal, and he asked me to come see him. On my arrival at his office, he told me that he and the faculty would like to have Dena and me stay at Columbia Academy. He said that we could live in the dorm there, and he would personally see that I got a good job so that I could pay my bill. Dena and I talked it over and decided that it sounded good to us, and agreed to stay. They hired both of us to be monitors in the dormitory, and I also did a lot of cleaning.

Mother and Ervin sold the cows and horses and moved to Meadow Glade so my brother wouldn't have so far to go to school. They rented an old house just down the lane from the school. Again there was a "little house' out back, but at least it had a drain board in the kitchen and a sink. On the drain board sat a small hand pump that sometimes needed priming with a glass of water to get the flow started.

I enjoyed living in the dormitory and made new friends. I also discovered a new phenomenon—homesick girls. I had never heard of such a thing as homesickness, though I had been bumped around a great deal. But I had never let myself have those feelings. I had always simply accepted the loneliness and rejection as part of life. *Maybe later!*

1944

While I was living in the dormitory, Dena came to me one day and said, "Roen, the man that you think is your father isn't really your father!"

"What? How do you know?" I exclaimed.

"Your Aunt Gertie and your Aunt Emma told me," she replied.

"Why did they tell you and not me?" I gasped.

"Your mother made them promise not to tell you, but they thought that you should know," she replied.

I was devastated, the pain coursing down my body from head to toe. Who to talk to? I knew that if I said anything to Mother about it, she would be angry. So I talked to the Lord about it a lot.

It hurt most that Mother had never told me. She'd led me to believe a lie. I hurt because my aunts had told my roommate and not me. I hurt because I had finally found a friend in Mamma Belle, and now to find out that Daddy wasn't even my real father. I began to understand why he had usually ignored me when I was younger and what a beautiful influence Mamma Belle had brought into my life.

My roommate went on to tell me that my real father's name was George Unselt—a name I had never heard before. How could I find out anything about him? What nationality was he? Was he still living? Did he have any other children? Was he a Christian? I needed answers!

But Mother refused to talk to me about it at all. She would say, "Quit feeling sorry for yourself." When I'd cry, she'd hit me, sometimes on my bottom, sometimes on my leg, sometimes on my arm or face. Often she would kick me when her temper flared. I still couldn't understand why my mother didn't like me. *If I could just talk to her about it*, I thought. I knew that she didn't treat Al and Cathie this way.

In February my sister arrived on the train with her three-month-old baby girl. She and her husband, Dick, had been living in Indiana, but Dick had now found someone else he preferred to live with, so he'd sent Cathie and Baby Cathie Lee to us. Oh, how I loved that baby! My sister needed to get a job, and since I got out of school at noon, my sister said that if I would move home and take care of Cathie Lee in the afternoons, she would help with my tuition. She found a neighbor who lived close by to care for her in the mornings.

I talked to Mother about it, and she and Ervin said that I could move to their house if I would do all the laundry and housework, plus care for the baby, and so forth. The girl's dean was very disappointed, because we had a good working relationship and she depended on me. I was 16 and almost at the top of the class. But I enjoyed Cathie Lee so much. I knew she was a gift from heaven.

We heated the house with a wood stove and used a wood-burning range in the kitchen for cooking and heating water. Often I would have to split more wood to fire up the stove. Then I'd pump water into the copper wash boiler, put it on the wood stove to heat, and then dump it into the old washing machine, which I had pulled out to the middle of the kitchen floor. Next I would get clean rinse water and run the clothes through it, before hanging them outside on the clothesline (if weather permitted). Otherwise I hung the diapers over a wooden rack and pulled it up in front of the open oven, where they dried pretty fast.

By the time the adults came home, I'd have dinner on the table, Cathie Lee would be cleaned, well loved, and cared for, and most of my homework would be done.

My stepfather became upset with me for some reason one day. I don't remember what the problem was, but he raked me over the coals, and I said, "I am really trying to get everything done." He looked at me in disgust and then spit out the words, "You aren't worth your salt!"

I was crushed. In my blurry, teenage vision I tried to correlate those hurtful words with his pious Christian philosophy, which refused me the right to curl my hair, because, he said, it was a sin. I really wanted to have curly hair, because all of the other girls did. They would put their hair up on rollers at night, and the next day their hair would look so pretty. I talked to Jesus a lot about this problem. And surprise! Soon my hair started to curl on its own! I could just wash my hair, run my fingers through it, and curls would appear. I knew it must be a direct gift from God.

Ervin also refused to let me wear silk or nylon hose, so I wore only brown, cotton hose, held up with a garter belt. I didn't like wearing them, and I felt that his demands were unreasonable.

I had so hoped that my mother would have an easier life after she married Ervin, but he never really worked and earned a living. He would try his hand at selling Christian books, door to door, but didn't make very much money at it, though it took a lot of his time.

So we often had to get by without enough food to eat. But I found that when I got invited over to a girlfriend's home that things were different there. They could go to the bathroom inside and take showers in private. In contrast, we bathed in a big, old, galvanized washtub that we put in the middle of the kitchen floor and, added warm water from the copper boiler, and each took a quick bath in once a week. It was often cold in the kitchen and there was no privacy.

Deep inside me I knew that it didn't always have to be this way. I took to heart the text that says, "I can do everything through Him who gives me strength" Philippians 4:13 *NIV*.

Chapter 6

Mamma Belle

1938-1987

I had now turned 17, and my heart and head were bursting to find out who my father *really* was and to trace my *real* roots. I had recently come home sick from college and was living with Mother and Ervin.

I had decided to confront Mother on the matter of my real father. One day we were standing in the hallway in front of the bathroom door, and I mustered up all the courage I had and said, "Mother, would you tell me about my birth father?"

She totally lost control, hit me in the face, kicked me in the legs, and screamed, "Don't you ever let me hear you speak of that again." Then she began to cry.

I wanted to comfort her, but she told me to get away from her. I felt so alone, so helpless. The Bible says to "Honor thy mother." I had to honor her wishes; I couldn't talk to her about this. But I now felt shut out of life, and it took a long time to process it all.

But my relationship with Daddy and his second wife, Mamma Belle, became special to me, and I didn't want to give it up. Yet I felt like a fake—after all, I wasn't Daddy's true daughter. I talked to my Friend Jesus, and He gave me comfort. He had helped me before, and I knew I could trust Him. I read my Bible and found solace in its promises, especially Romans 8:28: "All things work together for good to them that love God, to them who are called according to His purpose" *KJV.* I read my Bible all the way from cover to cover that year.

A few times Mamma Belle invited my sister and me to do something with Daddy and her or visit them for a short time in their Vallejo home, and I began to realize that each time she would always take each one of us aside for a short period of one-on-one time with her. One time she whispered in my ear, "Come here a minute, I want to show you something." She took me into her bedroom and showed me a lovely, black nightgown that one of her daughters had sent her. I had never been included like this with Mother. I tried to figure out what made this special, because I knew I loved it.

One day when I was at her home, she said, "I saw something down at the store and I think you would like it. Let's go look at it." When we got to the gift shop, I was amazed. I had never been in a place like it before. She took me over to a wall with two beautiful plaques of musicians and instruments, each about a foot high. She said, "Look at these, do you like them?" She saw me beaming from ear to ear and asked the clerk to wrap them up for me. I felt so very special.

Later on she died of emphysema, though she had never smoked, and I deeply regretted never having told her how special she was to me, or what a difference she had made in my life. I hope my confession here will inspire others—family, friends, or you—never to make the same mistake. So I am sharing these lines I so wish I had shared with her in life:

Dear Mom,

This letter is long overdue, but I just have to write. I was 10 years old when you married Daddy. Everything was so confusing. I really didn't know him very well, because he hadn't lived at home since I was four, and I had never had much of his time and felt lonely and neglected. Now he was married to a lady with nine children of her own.

I had never met you, but I began to think I would like to. I was shy, uncomfortable, jealous, and sad all at once. You never pushed yourself on me. When Daddy came to visit occasionally, he was usually alone, but once in a while he would bring some of your younger children. Little by little the hurts and resentments eased. I had heard that you were considerably older than Daddy, that you dyed your hair black, and that you had little education. Those things didn't seem to matter so much anymore.

I began to visit in your home occasionally. You always treated me as if I was special. You asked about my mother and acted like you really cared. You never criticized or complained. You always found occasion to do something special with me alone, even if it was just to go into your bedroom and shut the door—just the two of us—and show me some little treasure, maybe even a pretty little clip that you thought would be just right in my hair. Did you know you were melting my heart?

One time a friend came to visit and asked if I was your stepdaughter. You put your arm around me and your quick and positive response was, "Don't you let me hear you say that dirty word around here! This is our daughter."

Thank you so much for accepting my husband, Everett, into your heart and life. We were so happy that you were there when he graduated from medical school. You gave him a nice, new projector that he still uses and enjoys—27 years later.

You always made it a point to keep us posted on each of the children and grandchildren. Clearly we were your happiness. When our first child was born, you were ecstatic, even though he was, for you, grandchild number 35. When our second son was four months old, I became very ill and had to be hospitalized. The boys were 13 months apart, and we were at our wits end to find someone to care for them. I called you from the hospital, and you told me not to worry, that you would be there that night on the train. I will be forever grateful. You were 71 years old and not in the best of health. You stayed two weeks and insisted that you loved every minute spent with your grandsons.

Later, when we had five children, we made a trip to see you. I noticed that you made it a point to spend some time alone with each of them—a trip to the grocery store, a walk down the nearby railroad tracks, a private conference in the bedroom, a sandwich together in the backyard by the fishpond. Each time it was a special time with you. They each loved you dearly.

As I was convalescing from surgery later on, the doorbell rang, and when we opened the door, there stood Daddy and you. You had come 1,000 miles to see if everything was okay. I was overwhelmed. I confided to you that our oldest, now nine, desperately wanted a horse, but I shrugged my shoulders and said, "Maybe someday." There was certainly no room for a horse on our city lot. Your answer came through loud and clear: "Now you listen here, Honey, if you are ever going to do anything about it, do it now. Otherwise just hush up." I laughed and gave you a big hug. As soon as you left we followed your advice and started our search for a home in the country. We love this home, Mom; how we wish that you could have seen it before you went away.

The kids are grown and gone, the horses long since sold, but your influence in our lives will never leave.

All my love,

Your Daughter Roen

Daddy began to talk to me more. He never talked *about* me, how I felt, or my dreams—mostly about the family and how their lives were going. I wanted so badly to ask him about my heritage but could not muster the courage to bring it up.

He would write letters to me occasionally, and he would invite us to come visit him. He now treated me with love and respect.

Mary Margaret and Sam had each married two of Mamma Belle's older children, who'd since passed away. So Mary Margaret and Sam had married and remained closely connected to our family. Mary Margaret and Sam lived near Daddy, and they would check on him frequently to be sure he was all right. I called Daddy one time and Mary Margaret answered the phone. She said that Daddy was not doing well and that she didn't think he would live very much longer. At this time I was taking care of my son Daryl, who had been in an accident. But this was March, during Spring Break at the local college. I had been hiring a young man to come in and stay with Daryl once in awhile, and I decided to ask him if he would stay with Daryl during his Spring Break time so I could go see Daddy. He agreed.

I flew out of Portland, Oregon, for the short flight to Sacramento, California, on a Wednesday, about noon. Helen and Marv, lifelong friends, met me at the airport and took me to Daddy's apartment. They dropped me off and said to call if I needed anything. Mary Margaret and Sam were there. I encouraged them to go ahead and go home, that I would take good care of Daddy. They said, "Oh, we wouldn't go and leave you here alone with him." I could see that he wasn't doing very well, but I wanted so much to have a chance to talk to him and ask him about the burdens on my heart. They finally went out and sat on the porch to have a smoke. I wanted to ask Daddy about this George Unselt who was said to be my real father. I understood that Daddy and he had been friends at the same lodge. I wanted to tell him that I knew about all this and that I desperately needed some answers and appreciated all he and Mamma Belle had done for me.

As I was trying hard to figure out a way to approach the subject, the door opened and Mary Margaret and Sam came back inside. Mary said she was going to fix supper, so I volunteered to help her. Later, as we ate, I noticed that Daddy could hardly manage to get his food down. After we ate, he got up and shuffled toward the bedroom. He stopped and gave me a hug, and said, "Roen, thank you so much for coming, I really appreciate it, and I love you. Good night." It was the first time I remember Daddy ever telling me that he loved me. My heart swelled with joy.

He went to bed, set his alarm for 5 a.m., and fell asleep. I crawled under a blanket on the living room sofa and tried to sort it all out in my mind. How would I bring up this subject that hung so heavily on my heart? What would he say? Would he be angry? Was it fair to bring it up when he was so sick? I finally asked the Lord to work it out and drifted off to sleep.

I felt Mary Margaret shaking me, urgently telling me that she thought Daddy had passed away. It was 3 a.m. Would I come in and check on him? I tried hard to wake up. *Surely this must be a dream.* When I went in and put my fingers on Daddy's wrist, I couldn't find a pulse. Suddenly I came wide-awake. This was reality. I could tell that Daddy had moved to the side of the bed and tried to get up, before he'd collapsed back into bed and died.

I knew that Sam and my brother, Al, were named in Daddy's will to take care of his estate. But Sam didn't know where Daddy had put the written information about who to call in case of death. Quickly I called Al, and he told me who to contact and that he had that day off and would be with us in a couple hours. He was now a pilot for

United Airlines, and he was able to hop right onto a plane. I called the mortuary, and before we knew it there were lights flashing outside and someone was pounding on the door.

Sam opened the door and two policemen stood there. Several police cars were parked in front of the apartment, their lights flashing and their headlights all pointing toward our front door. They told us that a death had been reported and that they had come to check it out. We invited them in. They asked all sorts of questions and made out a report, then left. It wasn't long until the car from the funeral home came to pick up Daddy's body.

My brother, Al, arrived shortly at the Sacramento Airport and rented a car to drive up to Daddy's apartment in Auburn. He arrived at 7 a.m., and he and Sam immediately went out and bought 12 large cardboard boxes. After they got back, they unfolded the flattened boxes and lined them up in the living room. We then put each of the 12 children's names on them—nine of Mamma Belle's and three of Daddy and Mother's. Mamma Belle and Daddy had left lists of certain things that were to go to specific individuals and families. Most of the items on the lists were things we children had given them, and they wanted us to have them once they were gone. This part was easy to manage, because all the items were listed. But after that we had to start assigning things to various boxes, on our own.

That Wednesday afternoon we also started making funeral arrangements and notified all immediate family members. Since I absolutely had to be home by Sunday to take care of my son Daryl, we decided to have a graveside service on Saturday. Daddy had left instructions to have the lodge he belonged to take care of the services.

As we were cleaning out Daddy's apartment, I found hundreds of used, brown paper bags carefully folded and filed away inside other paper bags. I saved a few to use, and we made many trips to the dumpster to carry out the rest of them, along with many brown bags filled with folded newspapers. Daddy came from a generation that had gone through the Great Depression, where saving could mean survival.

Mary Margaret and Sam had gone home to freshen up and collect their wits. Al and I had packed up almost everything, and he was about ready to head back to San Francisco. Weariness set in, and I felt spooked about staying in Daddy's apartment alone that night. So I called my friends, Helen and Marv, who had picked me up at the airport, and asked if I could stay with them. They welcomed me warmly. I told them I could drive Daddy's car out to their place but needed directions, since I had never driven there myself. They insisted on coming and picking me up themselves, driving 45 minutes each way. It was so special to spend the evening and night with them, and a real comfort to me. The next morning they brought me back bright and early so I could help prepare for the funeral and greet family members as they arrived.

Our youngest son, David, phoned and told me he would be coming to help me at the funeral. On Saturday I kept hoping he would phone me to pick him up at the airport, but no call came. Finally I knew that if I didn't leave for the gravesite in Vallejo, I would be late. I felt keen disappointment, so alone. My husband, Everett, couldn't come; now none of my children would be there either. My Friend Jesus gave me courage and strength at that hard time. I thought about what 1 Corinthians 10:13 says, that He will make a way of escape, that ye may be able to bear it.

I had been to the cemetery before, with Daddy, to place flowers on Mamma Belle's grave. Now as I neared the gravesite, I saw my son David walking toward me. "How in the world did you get here?" I asked, overjoyed. "I was waiting for a call from you to pick you up, and it never came!"

He explained that in the rush of things he had bought a ticket into San Francisco Airport rather than Sacramento, so he had had to take a bus up from San Francisco. When he arrived at the Vallejo bus station, he'd asked for directions to the cemetery, and a stranger had spoken up and offered to drive him to the gravesite.

The service was brief and impersonal. The few family members that were there soon dispersed.

By then Daddy's apartment was beginning to look empty. On Saturday night, after the service, David and I went out and rented a truck. We picked it up Sunday morning and loaded it with the furniture that he wanted to take. Then he dropped me off at the Sacramento Airport in time for my flight home, before heading on down to Los Angeles. The next day Mary Margaret and Sam went in and finished cleaning out the apartment.

"And my God will meet all your needs according to His glorious riches in Christ Jesus" Philippians 4:19 *NIV. Thank you, Father in heaven.*

Mamma Belle and Daddy, 25th wedding anniversary

Mamma Belle and Roen, circa 1960

Chapter 7

On My Own

1945

*W*hen I graduated with honors from Columbia Academy, with my bill all paid up, I felt a great deal of satisfaction. I wanted to go to college and take nursing, and the way seemed to be opening when Vancouver Memorial Hospital hired me as a nurse's aide and Aunt Gertie, who lived within walking distance of the hospital, said I could live with her.

The hospital gave us new aides a five-day orientation course—something I needed as a naïve and bashful teenager. As the charge nurse assigned us our new duties, she said, "Bernard (my maiden name), you will be working on the men's floor." I couldn't believe it! My friends were snickering, because it had been a running joke, "What if they make us work on the men's floor!" I'd been saying that I was sure this could never happen, because after all, we were young girls. My face turned bright red.

As my charge nurse made rounds with us and gave us our assignments, she said, "Bernard, Mr. Jones will be your first patient. He needs an enema today." I turned even a brighter red, and I could hear my friends giggling. The four men in the ward started laughing, too. "Oh, look at her face!" they chortled. Somehow, with the Lord's help, I got through the day.

After a couple weeks an opening came in the obstetrical department. I loved babies, applied for the job, and got it. It was mostly an upbeat, happy place to work. Each day when walking to work, my feet flew. I liked my job, and I couldn't wait to see all those sweet babies and their happy mothers. I thought I could work there forever. One of the mothers named her baby girl after me. I was flattered, because I didn't know anyone else named Roen.

Packaged cotton balls and Q-tips where not yet available in those days, so the hospital would buy big rolls of cotton and have them made on site. Every free minute I would take a little wad of cotton, twirl it into a ball, and put it into a container, ready to be sterilized, or grab a special toothpick, accumulate a bit of cotton on the tip, and then twirl it around into a neat little Q-tip.

We had no disposable rubber gloves either, so I quickly learned to wash the used gloves thoroughly with soap and water, inside and out, before drying and powdering them and putting them into packets by pairs, ready to be sterilized. I liked to pop the fingers out.

The summer flew by. Walla Walla College sent me an acceptance letter, and because I had saved every penny all summer, except for my tithe (10 percent of my earnings), I had enough money to cover my entrance fees and some of my first-quarter expenses.

Dena and I moved into our room on the fourth floor of South Hall, two floors from the nearest bathroom and four floors from the front door. I qualified for Honors English class, which met on the second floor of the Ad Building, first thing in the morning. I would hurry down to ground level, then back up to English class. Wheezing and short of breath, I chided myself for being out of shape.

I found a job working for a Mrs. Whitehouse in the laundry, spending most of my time on the presses but learning enough about the whole operation to be able to fill in for any job. My work ethic stood me in good stead. Each week I worked about 40 hours. On Sunday mornings at 3 a.m., I would wheel a big cart around to the dormitories to pick up laundry, take it back to the plant, and have it sorted by the time the rest of the workers came in.

A full pre-nursing program at college kept me busy, and I played the cello in the orchestra. My worst problem was food. The school had a policy that each student must spend at least $18 a quarter at the cafeteria. I kept careful track of every penny I spent and adopted a routine of eating one cafeteria meal a day—sometimes breakfast, sometimes lunch, sometimes supper. I tried to rotate it, but I rarely ate healthful, well-balanced meals. I did eat a lot of Ruskets, which looked like rectangular pressed patties made out of extremely dry Corn Flakes without much flavor. I'd add milk and discovered that after eating this cereal, I didn't get hungry for a long time. The cafeteria served Ruskets every meal, every day (I found out later that Ruskets had made it on the list of non-rationed food during the war years).

My roommate, Dena, had an aunt and uncle who lived in the village, and usually once a week they invited us to their home for a meal. This was a big event, and I really appreciated it. Because I was overworked and undernourished, I was not thriving. I became very thin and tired, but within me the desire to succeed burned on.

1946

One Saturday night our orchestra presented a program in the auditorium. Afterward we sat for our picture, as an orchestra, for the yearbook, and I didn't get back to my room until 11:30. Since I had to be at work at 3 a.m., I decided that if I went to bed at 11:30, I probably wouldn't be able to wake up on time, and I didn't want to disturb my roommate by setting an alarm clock. So I gathered up my History of Nursing notes, went down to the parlor, and worked on a notebook that was due to be turned in soon.

By the time 3 a.m. came around, I was shivering, so I wore the heaviest coat I had and warm gloves. After I picked up the laundry, I stood sorting clothes, still wearing my coat and gloves. When Mrs. Whitehouse arrived for work, she looked me in the eye and asked, "What is wrong with you?" I said I was just cold. So she came over and felt my forehead, which was very hot. "You stop what you are doing right now, and go see the nurse," she told me. Though I was sick, it felt good that she cared. I did go to the nurse, and she took me right into her makeshift infirmary.

"You are really sick," she said. "We will keep you here where no one can come to see you, so you won't give anyone your germs."

The makeshift infirmary consisted of a room with a bathroom and a little sink. It was on the main floor in North Hall, and quite lonely. If only I had a mother who would come see me! *And how will I ever be able to pay my bills, spending all this time in bed and not working. And how am I ever going to get my class work made up?"* Such worries for a girl of only seventeen!

Somebody would bring my food at mealtime, and once a day the nurse would come see me; otherwise I was alone—well, not quite alone. I talked a lot to my Friend Jesus and found great comfort in Him.

On Sabbath afternoon, a friend who lived across the hall from me came down to the infirmary, with her fiancé. They ignored the "Do Not Enter" sign on the door and sat down to visit for a while. I was delighted to see someone I knew. I had met her fiancé at Thanksgiving time, when he drove up to take her the 240 miles from College Place, Washington, to Portland, Oregon, for the holiday. Otherwise I did not know Everett, but Betty was my friend, and I enjoyed talking to them. I felt a little smug that they had come in to see me and were willing to take the chance of getting sick themselves. Everett was in the army, stationed at Fort Lewis, and had come to visit Betty on the weekend.

In about a week my fever disappeared, and I began to feel better and anxious to get back to work, so I could pay my bills. The nurse agreed that I could go back to school, so I plunged right into my studies and went right back to work, as many hours as I could. The College had no counseling system in place for students, back then, and I certainly was not receiving any advice from home.

Two days later my fever shot up again and I felt dreadful. I went again to see the nurse, and she sent me to the doctor, who put me in the hospital. That was really scary. *How in the world would I pay a hospital bill? What have I done?*

The doctor ordered penicillin shots—a fairly new drug on the market back then—every two hours. The shots made me very sore, and I felt really lonely. I no longer seemed to have any control over my life, and I was very, very discouraged. I stayed in the hospital a week. My discharge orders were to get lots of rest and not to work for a while. I just knew that I would have a huge hospital and doctor bill, and my school bill wouldn't get paid. I had no health insurance.

I wrote to my mother and told her that I wasn't able to pay my bills. She sent me just enough money for a bus ticket and said I should come to their home, get a job, and take care of my bills that way. So I packed up my belongings, told my roommate and friends goodbye, and left. *What now?* I asked my Heavenly Father.

When I arrived home, my stepfather made it clear that I would be living by *his* rules. Mom and Ervin were living in a place called Vanport, between Vancouver and Portland, and by now owned a car, but Ervin told me that they would not provide any transportation for me. Bus service was available, but their apartment was far away from stores and businesses. Vanport consisted largely of apartments, built in eight-plexes, as short-term housing. My parents had a two-bedroom unit, but the room my brother, Al, and I stayed in was stacked to the ceiling with household goods that wouldn't fit elsewhere.

I gained strength, and Mother told me about a job that would soon open at our church headquarters, where she worked. She said I should apply. I got the job and felt very thankful, because now I could pay off my bills. But when I received my final bill from the college, I was amazed to discover that I actually had a $60 credit. If only someone at the college had provided some counseling, I probably could have stayed and finished out the year.

About this time I received a letter from my sister, Cathie. Some time before she had returned with their little girl to her estranged husband Dick, in response to his pleading. She was now seven months pregnant with his child, but Dick had decided that he really preferred living with his "Sweetie," instead of Cathie. "Sweetie," as it turned out, was also seven months pregnant with his child.

So he put Cathie, their little girl Cathie Lee, and all their belongings on a train to Portland and sent them to me. Cathie arrived hungry and penniless, owing extra freight charges for her belongings. I paid those charges and got her things released. Mother and Ervin, meanwhile, had moved to California, so they weren't available to help in any way.

I helped Cathie make arrangements to rent a house in a housing project called McLaughlin Heights, across the river in Vancouver. We were now in the post-World War II housing boom, when hurriedly built housing was going up for low-rent occupants. Cathy talked to a social worker and found that limited assistance was available. Her rent would be paid each month, but she would receive nothing for food, furnishings, and other necessities.

My earnings were now $118 a month, working at the church headquarters, so on payday I would cash my check, take out money for carfare, pay my tithe, and give the rest to Cathie. We weren't living luxuriously, but we were able to make ends meet and were thankful for God's love and care. I dearly loved my little niece and newborn nephew, Terry, and wanted the best for them.

We attended church in Vancouver, and I was asked to be youth leader. I enjoyed the assignment, because I liked to do whatever I could to help young people. The church planned to send local delegates to a youth congress in San Francisco and told me that if I would serve as a delegate, they would pay for my transportation. It sounded good to me, until I found out that I could not get the time from my job. How I longed to see my old friends in the Bay Area. *Maybe another time!*

From time to time I would run into Everett, my friend Betty's now ex-fiancé. She had written to tell me that she had broken up with him because she thought they should both date around for a while. She hoped I'd go see him, because he'd injured his head in a very bad accident. His face was now deeply scarred from going through a windshield, so she hoped I would encourage him. I wasn't about to do that, but when I would see him at church activities or happen to meet him here and there, we would talk. In time he started phoning me at work, inviting me to go on little outings.

Once he asked me to go on a hike with him up to Multnomah Falls, along the Columbia River east of Portland. On that hike I slipped and fell, making a small hole in a knee of my nylons. I was concerned! I needed to wear nylons to work, and if these were ruined, I didn't know when I would be able to get any more.

A few days later Everett showed up with a big smile at my work, with a little package in his hand. Sure enough, it was a pair of nylons. I wasn't very interested in him romantically, but it was nice to have a friend who thought I was special. So from time to time he and I would get together, and I always tried to include my sister and the kids, because I didn't want them to be stuck at home alone. So when he would call and ask if I would go to a meeting with him, I would say, "Fine, can I take my sister and the kids?" And he would say, "Sure." He was pretty generous that way, and they liked him.

One day I was waiting for him to come pick us all up, and a friend of his came by and told us, "Everett didn't have enough money for gas, so he asked me to come pick you up for him." I said, "Oh, really? He didn't say anything to me about that."

We were kind of stalling around, wondering if this was for real or not, when I mentioned, "My sister and the kids are going with us." Since he had a two-door coupe, we tried to figure out a way to get everybody inside. Seat belts were unheard of in cars back then, so it was simply a matter of fitting everybody in. As he danced around, stomping from one foot to another, waiting for us to get ready to go, up drove Everett. I invited him in and he looked quizzically at his friend, Charles, then at us.

"Charles said that you couldn't come because you didn't have enough money for gas," I volunteered. "He said that you had asked him to come get us."

Everett knew that Charles was a practical joker, so he quickly picked up on the ruse. Charles had driven clear over from Portland just to pull this prank. All in all, we had fun with Everett and his friends. If we'd had a phone, it would have been easier to make plans and change them when needed.

Even though I liked my work at the church headquarters and made many friends there, I knew I needed to give my sister more financial help. One day a Dr. Nelson phoned our office, and since I was the receptionist, I answered the call. "This is Dr. Nelson," he said, "and I am a heart specialist associated with Portland Adventist Hospital. I'm wondering if you know of anyone who wants a job as secretary. I need someone to do the transcribing, greet patients, and make appointments."

"Let me take your number and I'll get back to you," I offered. "I might know of somebody."

When I got home, I talked to my sister about it and said, "I think this might be an opportunity, what do you think? The pay is better and I would enjoy that kind of work. Even if I can't go to school and be a nurse, I can still work in the medical field. Do you think I should do it?"

"You can always interview for it," she suggested.

I found Dr. Nelson's office in downtown Portland, at the Medical Arts Building. The long, tedious ride to my old job would be shortened if I worked here, and I wouldn't have to transfer buses.

When I interviewed for the job, Dr. Nelson and his assistant took an immediate liking to me, and I felt the same about them. He hired me, and I gave notice at the church headquarters. It was very helpful to have a little more money each month.

Cathie, Roen, Mother, Al, circa 1980

Standing: David, Debra
Seated, Daryl, Diane,
Duane. Roen made the
twins and Diane's outfits,
circa 1966

Everett, Jack Bailey's "King for
a Day," circa 1953

Winter wonderland, our
English Cotswold home,
circa 1960

50th wedding anniversary 1997

Roen on her Honda 350

Roen, Everett, Daryl, circa
1998

Roen the realtor, circa 1994

Roen, water aerobics at the "Y,"
circa 2002

Daryl and his "service dog"
Icon, circa 1980

Daryl, circa 1979, on the
raft trip

Daryl, taken by Diane just before he left on his fateful trip, August 1, 1978

Daryl on the raft trip

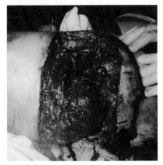

Daryl's leg after the accident

Duane, Daryl, Diane, Everett and Snowball, circa 1964

Everett attended a Christian college in downtown Portland. Although he would have preferred to go to Walla Walla College, he had just been discharged from the army and was still recovering from an auto accident. He would get horrible headaches and didn't really want to go away to college yet. The college in Portland just happened to be a few blocks from where I worked.

We started eating our sack lunches together, and on nicer days we would meet at the benches in front of the public library, across from where I worked. Then I would go back to work and he would return to school.

Everett's headaches seemed to be easing up, but sometimes he was overwhelmed with pain, and I asked my girlfriend what she thought about dating a person who had such severe headaches. She said I should be concerned, because these attacks might be something lifelong or perhaps worse. She thought I should not get into a situation where I might be the sole breadwinner. I decided to let my Best Friend lead in the matter!

I prayed a lot about our friendship. I knew we were both still young, and I vowed that whatever I did, I would not let my family deteriorate as my parents had done. I asked the Lord to direct our relationship.

The church rented the roller skating rink once a month, and Everett often took me to skate. After work we'd meet, go skating, and then he'd take me home. It was quite an imposition on him, I thought, because he lived 30 miles from my house. Then, as our relationship grew, we began to date more seriously and realized we had deep feelings for each other.

One day I asked him where he was going to college the next year. He said he wanted to go to Walla Walla College. As a veteran, he had some GI Bill benefits that would help with his tuition and provide a small living stipend.

He then told me that he loved me, but that he didn't feel that it was fair to ask any girl to go through what he was planning to go through—four years of college, four years of medical school, plus an internship and residency. I told him that I loved him and would be willing to help him reach his goal. We decided to pray about it, and see what the Lord had in mind.

I explained to him that I wanted to help my sister and didn't want to abandon her and her precious children, but I was open to change. My sister already had a boyfriend, and in time they were married, so my assistance was not needed anymore. Everett and I finally concluded that we should marry at Christmastime and move to Walla Walla College the following June.

We left it in God's hands, claiming Proverbs 3:6: "In all your ways acknowledge Him, and He will make your paths straight" *NIV*.

Chapter 8

Sharing Forever

1947

*E*verett got a $5,000 settlement from his auto accident, took the money, and bought a tiny trailer, 15 feet long and eight feet wide. But it was new, and fairly nice, though it had no water heater, bathroom, or refrigerator. But it did have an icebox.

My mother and her husband had told me they could not help me with any wedding expenses, and I'd been saving a little money as a wedding fund. My Aunt Rosie let me borrow her wedding dress, and though it was the wrong size, she gave me permission to take in the seams as long as I didn't cut the fabric itself. A friend loaned me her veil and a white Bible, and Everett bought an orchid for me to carry on the Bible.

Then he and I went out into the woods and cut sword ferns to tie to an archway in the church. When we finished decorating the archway, it looked very pretty. We found that the church owned two large baskets, and we filled them with displays of holly, which a church member let us cut from her yard. It set the tone for a lovely Christmas-day wedding.

I sewed some pretty underwear and nightgowns for myself, using fabric from some too-large used clothing someone had given me. I added touches of embroidery on them and a little lace when I could find it. Finally, I carefully sewed snaps on the panties. They were beautiful!

The wedding itself was simple. The men in the ceremony wore whatever suits they happened to have. Everett's suit came from Bob Sanders' parents—they'd given it to him when Bob had outgrown it. The ladies wore whatever formalwear they had or could borrow. One of my bridesmaids didn't own a long dress, so someone gave me a dress that I lengthened and altered to fit her. I went to the market in Portland and bought bunches of chrysanthemums to make nosegays for the bridesmaids to carry, corsages for family members, and boutonnieres for the men. A church member taught me how to fix the flowers and helped me get ribbon for a good price. I skipped my family's Christmas get-together, which gave me time to work with the flowers. Someone made us a wedding cake for $20, and family members agreed to serve it with the punch at the reception.

Several weeks before the wedding, I phoned my mother in California from Vancouver. I told her I was planning to get married and that I would like to have her come to the wedding.

"Oh, I can't possibly do that," she replied.

"I still have $50 and that would pay for your bus fare. If you'll come, I'll send it you so that you can be here," I offered.

Then she said simply, "No, I won't come."

Once again I was crushed. She didn't say she was sorry. She didn't send a letter or a card. She obviously didn't want to be part of my life. It hurt. Neither Mother nor my stepfather ever sent money or a gift of any kind, or even asked if we needed any help. Even though I was getting married, I still wanted my mother to accept me.

Daddy arrived on Christmas day, alone, because Mamma Belle assumed that my mother would be at the wedding, and she didn't want to make Mother uncomfortable. Daddy walked me down the aisle and gave me a clothing iron as a gift; Mamma Belle sent along a pretty silk slip. I wanted so much to ask Daddy about my birth father, but I couldn't bring myself to spoil the moment. Everyone in my mother's family still refused to talk to me about it.

After the reception Everett and I went to the trailer. I felt embarrassed taking off my clothes in front of Everett, so I gave my clothes a yank over my head and in the process whammed my arms right into the ceiling. We laughed about that. That first night we parked our trailer in a park near the Columbia River.

That was Thursday night, and on Friday morning we drove down to Seaside to spend two nights before going back to get settled for work and school. I doubt the little motel where we rented a room for $10 had housed many honeymooners. We got a break on the price, and early Sunday morning we drove home. We loved the nice gifts our friends and family had given us, and as we found a place for each item, we were filled with excitement and love. Everett had a term paper to write, so even though school didn't begin for another two weeks, he was busy. I was busy too, returning to work that Monday.

On Memorial Day Weekend, 1948, we went to the beach to get away. While we were there, we heard on the radio that the Columbia River was flooding. Since our trailer wasn't very far from the river, we headed straight for home. On the way we kept tuned in to the radio and learned that the flooding was serious. As we approached our trailer park, we could see that other trailers had just been moved to our park from locations closer to the river—into any available spot, reserved or not, to get them out of harm's way. The water never reached our trailer, but life was a mess for a while because we had no place to park our car, and the court's washroom and shower rooms were overcrowded.

Everett's classes would be starting soon at Walla Walla College, where he planned to major in physics. A friend named Nellie wanted to ride with us as far as Walla Walla, on her way to Spokane, Washington, and we said "Sure." So we hooked our trailer up and set out, unaware that the flood had made much of the Columbia River Gorge Highway impassable. As it turned out, we had to veer far south, into central Oregon, to get around the damage and on to Walla Walla. It was a long, hard, dirty trip. Everything we owned was in this little trailer behind us, and most of the roads we were traveling were new to us. We felt like we were sort of wandering around.

We finally reached our destination and parked our trailer in a court owned by the college. Then we drove Nellie to Spokane, so she could meet with her family there. On our way back from Spokane, we got lost and had a little spat because I wasn't a very good navigator.

I'd never driven a car and I didn't know a lot about reading maps. I figured you just rode along, kept your mouth shut, and got where you were going. Everett said, "Can't you even read a map?" I said, "Sure, I can read a map, but I don't know which way to read it!" It was kind of a trial time, so we decided to pray about it. We had no idea where we were, out there in farm country. There were no stations, no signs, and all I had was a piece of paper, and my husband expected me to tell him where to go. You know what? I've learned to read maps since then, which is a good thing. We finally got out of that mess, thanks to our loving, Heavenly Father. We decided it just wasn't worth having a spat over.

The challenge of finding a job now loomed for me. Everett's classes would start soon, and he would try to find something to do part time. I thought I wouldn't have any problem finding a job in a doctor's office, but no luck. I looked and looked and tried and tried.

Then I found an ad in the paper saying that a nurses' aide was needed at the St Mary's Hospital in Walla Walla. I interviewed for the job and got it. My working hours were 11:00 p.m. to 7:00 a.m., and I loved the work. I'd had three months experience and one week of "training" in the nurse's aide department after I graduated from high school. I liked the registered nurse I now worked with. We had 30 to 40 patients under our charge, 10 of them pediatric patients, so we had a lot of work. I didn't get sleepy very often, working those hours, because I was busy all the time. I liked the work and especially enjoyed the kids in pediatrics.

As weeks passed, I began to realize that the trailer park where we lived in our trailer with its very thin walls and windows was exceptionally noisy during the daytime, while I was trying to sleep. Most of the people who lived there had children, and the kids would play outside during the day. I began to feel really tired and thought that maybe I should look around for a day job. An ad I found said that the Corps of Engineers, based in Walla Walla, was hiring, so I went in for an interview and they hired me to work in the stenographers' pool. They found that when they needed extra work done, I was usually willing and able to do overtime, so I stepped right up the ladder and was loaned out early on to the cost-accounting department.

Everett often told me about what he was learning in college, and our conversations often centered entirely on his schoolwork. He didn't have a clue how to reach into my heart and talk about my feelings and dreams, and I didn't know how to express myself on those matters, either. We were goal-centered, and we were both determined to get there.

I had very little time to myself to pursue any hobbies or interests. I liked to read, and reading didn't interrupt his studies. I liked self-help books, personal stories, and above all the Bible.

Everett came in one day and suggested that we become ham radio operators. I had no idea what he was talking about, but he patiently explained that it would be a way to communicate with each other and others around the world. We would learn a lot, he said, and it would be fun to do together. That part sounded good to me, so I agreed. We went to classes held at one of the public schools, and we both got our Amateur Radio Licenses in 1948. His call was W7OYU; mine was W7OYR. He built a ham radio set for us, a large, unsightly piece of equipment, but the transmitter had 450 watts of power. We sat it on the only place available—a small shelf at the head of the bed. The receiver was smaller, but still took up most of the remaining space. It left just enough room for our amateur radio log and our Bible. Soon I was talking to people in Japan and around the world. Everett hung up a little 10-meter antenna, and it worked. It was really the only thing I did for fun. I would talk on the radio primarily on Sundays, while he was studying at the library. Then he got hold of two smaller transmitters on which we could talk to each other, and anyone else who was a "ham" locally. It proved to be handy, since we had no telephone.

An opportunity came for me to learn how to use the bookkeeping machine at work—a machine that predated electronic calculators and computers. The engineers were working on a lot of hydroelectric dam projects, and they kept separate ledger sheets for each project. I had to slip the ledgers into the back of this machine and put in all the information, from a massive bank of keys, in addition to a typewriter keyboard. When I'd finish inputting data, I'd push the right button and everything would print out on the page. I kept the ledger sheets in a file beside my desk.

The other bookkeeping machine operator was Alice. She knew what she was doing, and she helped me a lot. In time I became really good on the machine, so I spent most of my time working there; however, for overtime I went to whatever department needed help and pitched in and did whatever I was asked to do. Alice and I got along well together. The bookkeeping machines we operated were pretty noisy, so they put the two of them in a very small room and kept the door closed so it wouldn't bother the other workers. Alice was a chain smoker and I didn't like the smoke, but I didn't want to complain. I don't think it was good for my lungs.

I was busy concentrating on my work one day when Alice wanted to get my attention, so she flipped a paperclip at me. It landed in my machine, which promptly refused to work anymore. At first we laughed about it, but then we felt terrible. We didn't want to have to get a repairman to come over or to get behind in our work.

So I told Alice that I thought I could fix it. I dismantled the machine, got the paperclip out, and put it back together, and hooray, it worked! Some of Everett's ingenuity must have rubbed off on me.

I liked the idea that our trailer was new and nice, but I didn't care for living in such a small space. Small spaces gave me claustrophobia. The walls offered no place to hang pictures, because they all had little cupboard doors on them. Two of the winters we spent there were extremely cold, and the little propane heater couldn't keep it warm enough. Sometimes ice would accumulate on the inside of the walls, freezing our blankets to the wall because the upper part of the trailer would be sweating with heat, trickling condensed moisture down onto the bed.

One very cold night my feet felt like they were freezing, so I heated some water to the boiling point on the stove and filled the hot water bottle. We stuffed it into the foot of the bed and then both jumped in. All of a sudden I screamed, and we both jumped out of bed. The heat had melted the neck right out of the hot water bottle. What a revelation on how wet one little water bottle can make a bed! We had a plastic tablecloth, so we turned the mattress over and put the tablecloth between the mattress and box springs. We piled the wet sheets and blankets on the floor, remade the bed, and climbed in. The next morning I took the wet bedding out to the washroom and dried it all in the dryer. We turned the mattress up and put the heat on high to dry it.

Everett's birthday was February 2. It was cold and icy outside, and I baked and decorated a cake for him and left it sitting in the middle of the table. I wanted him to see it when he first came in. The table hooked into the wall and had a leg that folded down to the floor to support it. When the leg was folded up, the table slanted clear down to the floor.

As Everett stepped inside, the ice on the bottom of his shoes caused him to slip and fall on the trailer floor, kicking the leg out from under the table. As he fell, he grabbed for the cake, but wound up with nothing but a handful of gooey frosting and a bit of cake. By the time I stepped in, the cake was upside down on the floor with my husband. Everett looked up at me with pain in his eyes and said, "Darling, it's a beautiful cake." I burst into gales of laughter. He didn't really like cake anyway.

"A cheerful look brings joy to the heart, and good news gives health to the bones." Proverbs 15:30 *NIV.*

Roen, graduation 1945

Everett, graduation 1945

Daryl, circa 1982

Roen and Everett, December 25, 1947

Our care home where Daryl lives

The gardenia Everett bought Roen for their first anniversary was frozen solid just two minutes after he gave it to her, due to the cold College Place, Washington weather.

Chapter 9

Loss and Readjustments

1948

*J*ust before Thanksgiving, a courier brought a message to Everett in class. He read it and dashed out to phone me: "You have got to come home now!" he implored. "Tell your carpool riders to find another way home, we are going to Portland!"

While he caught his breath, I told him I could tell he was hurting and asked what had happened. He told me that one of his parents' neighbors, a Dr. Smith, had called to report that he had answered a frantic call for help from Everett's mother, and when he arrived at her home, he'd found her in hysterics, standing beside a dirt-moving machine that had pinned her husband across the chest with its massive bucket.

Dr. Smith had examined Everett's father then and there and confirmed the worst—the machine had crushed out his life. The Fire Department later removed the body.

I made a quick exit from work, wondering all the way home what I could say to help ease my husband's heartache. Even the Bible texts that came to my mind seemed distant and inadequate. With heavy hearts we jumped into the car and headed for Portland.

Everett's dad had built the machine himself, for his dirt-moving business. Its big front bucket could move a yard of dirt at a time. The accident had occurred when he'd elevated the bucket to work on some mechanical parts underneath and then had evidently tripped a lever that let the bucket down, pinning him. Everett's mother had seen her husband drive into the yard earlier, but he hadn't come into the house for some time, so she'd gone out see how he was doing. When she'd found him pinned by the machine, she'd called for help.

After we arrived in Portland, somehow we worked our way through the preparations and funeral service. My father-in-law had been only 48. It didn't make sense that he should die. Everett's sisters were so young and their young hearts were crushed. Mother Wilson seemed to have aged years in those few, short days, and she asked me to take her shopping to buy a black dress. She dealt with her breaking heart and fears as best she could and found comfort in having her son with her.

Everett's two sisters were only 3 and 11 years old. After the tragedy, Mother Wilson wanted to move away from the old place and its memories, but she had never worked for hire and didn't have any skills. She didn't know what do. They had lived in the lower level of this Depression-era house on 59th and Stark Street for at least 10 years, paying $15 a month rent for the apartment and the big back yard, where Everett's father stored his dirt-moving equipment, tools, and all sorts of metal things he thought he might use someday.

The house consisted of just three rooms—a kitchen, a bathroom, and a bedroom. The bathroom had a claw-foot tub, and from wall to wall over the tub they'd stretched a rope. This they used for a closet. Papers, clothes, and other things were stacked everywhere. Other than a small pantry, they had no closets or cupboards. Under the drain board Father Wilson had installed a few rough shelves, and Everett's mother had put up a curtain to hide the shelves. The top of the drain board was covered with bottles, glasses, dishes, and other kitchen-related items. There was no refrigerator, and heat came only from a small wood stove in the bedroom and a cook stove in the kitchen. Everett's mother baked a lot of bread and pies in it and didn't complain. There was no life insurance, and she had nothing of monetary value except her car. She had no income source at all, and they had been living hand to mouth.

In talking things over with me, Everett suggested that he quit school and use his father's equipment to support all of us. I didn't want Everett to quit school—this was his opportunity to get an education. I suggested that instead we ask Mother if she and the girls would like to come and live with us. We did, and she said she would like that. She owned a '39 Mercury, and between that and our car, we were able to load in enough of their clothes and necessities for a month's visit to Walla Walla.

Let me tell you how it was living with five of us in that little trailer. There was no storage space, so we used the car for storage. We let Everett's mother and the two girls use our bed, which was a bit smaller than a normal double bed. It reached across the back end of the trailer, wall to wall; the built-ins encroached on the open space on either end of the bed, leaving enough room for two people to sit side by side. The three of them slept crowded in our bed.

In the front end of the trailer, next to the collapsible table, two padded seats lined the wall on either side, where two people could sit if they sat cozy. Those two seats opened into a very small bed, and here Everett and I slept. It was a trial and a nuisance, because we had to pull the table out and make up the bed every night and put it back together every morning.

With so many people living in that small space, I cannot describe how it looked, and how I felt. I told Everett, "We have got to do something. We need to find a place for them to live, because this isn't going to work for long." He said, "How are they ever going to be able to afford to live any place else? They don't have any income."

I replied, "I wonder if your mother would be interested in doing some housework. That wouldn't take a lot of training." So we talked to her about it and she said she, "Yes, I would." So I checked around and helped her find housekeeping jobs, some of which she held for several years.

We lived together in the trailer for a little more than a month, then we went back to Portland to clean out Mother's apartment and bring the rest of the family's things. Studying in the trailer was now impossible for Everett, so he spent many hours at the library. When I wasn't at work, I tried to spend quality time with Mother Wilson and the two girls. They were sweet and we all loved each other, but it was difficult. In that little trailer, if even one thing was left out of place, everything looked messy. I knew that somehow God had a plan for all of us, and would see us through.

We had $3,000 in our savings account, which we had carefully saved to apply toward eventual medical school expenses. But now we needed to find a place for them to live. I'd noticed a small, garage-like building on the back of a lot, which had temporarily been used as a dwelling, while the occupants planned to build a new house out front—but the new home never materialized. So now the modified garage with its one bathroom, kitchen, and small bedroom stood vacant. If Mother Wilson and the girls could live there, they would be able to raise a garden, too, I thought. So I inquired about the structure and land and found out that $3,000 would buy it outright. I swallowed hard and said, "Okay, let's buy it for her." She smiled from ear to ear.

At Christmastime we drove back to Portland in our car to clean out the flat and load Mother Wilson's things into the back of a 1935 Ford dump truck that had belonged to Everett's father. The glass was broken out of the truck's passenger-side window, and as Everett and I drove it through rain, snow, and freezing temperatures on our way to Walla Walla, things became almost unbearable. *The truck was old, ugly, and what if Everett really did quit school and try to make a living driving this heap?* We'd hooked the dirt-mover behind the truck, and both vehicles were stacked high with household items as we made our way toward Walla Walla. Mother drove our car with the girls.

Everett had worked with his father in the earth-moving business during high school and his first year of college. He always thought he could make a success of the business, and frequently reminded me that if he couldn't make it in college, he could always move dirt. I didn't like to hear him talk that way. I had nothing against people who moved dirt for a living, but I did not want to live the rest of my life like his parents had lived theirs. I knew they just barely got by. Of course I had lived like that most of my own life already, but I wanted something better and knew that we had an opportunity and that we needed to take it.

When we arrived in College Place, we parked the dump truck and the loader on the property beside the little house and helped Mother and the girls settle in. We were all tired, dirty, and hungry. Everett and I then went back to our little trailer, and it felt so good to be there, just the two of us. We took showers at the washhouse and then climbed into our own bed. I didn't mind having his family, but it was hard, and I thanked the Lord for this blissful moment.

We now began to replenish our savings account. Sometimes I worked up to 20 hours overtime each week and got paid time-and-a-half. That summer, Everett worked at whatever he could find to do, hoeing weeds around poles for Bonneville Power Administration, picking peaches, and helping put up metal buildings. He was versatile and adaptable. He never sat around.

Everett wanted to fix up a car, sell it, and use the money to buy a more dependable car for us. He was sure that if he bought a junker and fixed it up nicely, he could sell it for a profit and buy a better one, so he went ahead and bought a second car before selling the old one.

It was a very cold winter and we had no garage, but Everett felt that he couldn't afford antifreeze for both cars. One night the weather was exceptionally cold, so he went out to start the cars to keep their engines from freezing up. When he came back in, he brought the devastating news that the blocks of both cars had cracked. He had tried to drain all the water out of one of the engines, but some residual water had remained, and when the water froze, the surrounding metal cracked, ruining the engine.

So he scurried around that winter and found two wrecked cars with good blocks, bought the blocks, and installed them in our cars. This caused a lot of stress, as we poured money, time, and emotion into these cars. As soon as he got them running, he sold one and put antifreeze in the other. We'd learned a lesson about false economy.

1949

Our second summer at Walla Walla College, Everett decided he should go to Valsetz, Oregon, where his grandparents lived, to work in the woods—it was his best opportunity to make money, he believed. I didn't like the idea too well, because my job would not permit me to go with him. So I asked my sister and her two children to come and visit for a while.

Meanwhile, Everett had been teaching me to drive. I didn't really like the way he taught me, because he was always telling me what I was doing wrong, and I wanted him to like the way I did things. I now had a permit, so I decided to surprise him when he got back and have my license. My sister would be my teacher. We practiced a lot.

The day my sister and I went to the Department of Motor Vehicles, I nervously walked up to the counter with all my identification, prepared to take my driving exam. The woman at the window looked at my documents and said, "You are only 20 years old, so you will have to have your parents sign for you." I proudly pulled out my marriage license and gave it to her. "Oh, then your husband will have to sign for you!" she said. I was flabbergasted—confused, angry, crushed, and disappointed, all at once.

When Everett got back, I told him about my adventure at the DMV, and I think it made him feel very important! When I asked him to go with me to get my license, what could he say?

A very large man in a sheriff's uniform took me out for the test drive, while Everett waited at the office. The officer asked me to pull into a rather tight spot along the road, which I did. Then he said, "Now, back down the road 20 feet." So I put the car in reverse, gave it some gas, and it just sat there. It wouldn't move! I tried again and glanced over at the examiner. I could see that his face was getting red. There was no way to turn around.

Finally he loudly ordered me to drive back to the office. I had to jump a curb and drive over some rough ground to get turned around, and when I again looked over at him, his face was beet red. I finally got back on the road and headed for the office.

"The very idea of your husband's sending you out to take a test in a car that won't back up," he growled. I was sure I wouldn't get a license for a long time now.

When I pulled into the DMV, I made sure to park so that I wouldn't have to back up when I left. As we went into the office, Everett stood at the door to meet us. His smile quickly faded when he saw the examiner, who quickly and loudly shouted, "What kind of a scum would send his wife out to take a driving test in a car that won't even back up?" Everett couldn't believe what he was hearing. The car had never refused to back up before. I hadn't shed a tear yet, but wished I could. Crying was not something I usually could do. As usual, I stuffed it. *Maybe next time!*

This problem with the car was one more thing to distract Everett from his studies, but he always figured out a way to make things work. Somehow he got the gears unstuck, and we didn't have any more problems with the transmission. As soon as we were confident that the car would function properly, we went back to the DMV. I thanked my Heavenly Father that a different examiner ran me through this test, and I got my license without a hitch.

Everett prides himself on his ability to select and work on used automobiles. He can usually figure out the cause of a problem and fix it. I think he considers every car a work of art. He liked the design of our '46 DeSoto, but sometimes it would stall in the middle of the road, especially at stop signs. Everett figured out that if he hit the engine in a certain spot with a broomstick, it would restart, so he kindly sawed off an old broomstick, took me out to the car, and showed me where to hit the engine if it stalled. Then he securely stowed the stick under the hood.

I carpooled to work with three people, to save us all money. One afternoon, during rush hour, I was driving the DeSoto in downtown Walla Walla when we pulled up to the stoplight in front of the Whitman Hotel—and there it happened! The car just died. So I jumped out, knowing that the light wouldn't stay red for long. One of the male riders, sitting in the passenger seat in front, called out to me in dismay, "What are you doing?" But I kept moving, raised the hood, grabbed the stick, and started whacking at the engine. The women in the back seat started laughing, thinking I'd gone berserk. But then I slammed the hood back down and ran for the driver's-side door amid much horn-honking. Everybody in the car was laughing, so I joined them. And yes, I was praying all the time. Do you hear me, Jesus? I need help! I twisted the key and the engine started right up.

Our trailer was situated under a big black walnut tree, and the tree created quite a mess to walk in around our house. So we kept an eye open for some used bricks, and I was pleased when someone offered a bunch of them to us if we would just haul them away. Everett helped me make a little brick walkway right up to the front door. I also planted a few flowers, and in summertime it looked quite attractive, though barren in winter.

A long boardwalk in our trailer court ran between two rows of trailers over to the washhouse. It was about two and a half feet wide and got pretty slippery in the wintertime. We had been given two teakettles as wedding gifts, and these were invaluable, because we didn't have hot water in the trailer. I could take them both to the washhouse and bring back enough warm water in them to do the dishes—it saved butane.

One day I grabbed both of the teakettles, one in each hand, and stepped onto the walk. The next thing I knew my feet were stretched out behind me, and I was skidding along that walk on two teakettles! I thought I'd damaged the pots beyond repair, but again Everett came to my rescue. He got both of them straightened out enough to use.

I disliked going out to the shower room with its cold, concrete-gray floors in winter. I made my visits there as short as possible and vowed someday to have a better life.

We both felt refreshed after going to church each week, and we had worship and prayed together at home. We knew that getting into medical school would be difficult. A lot of veterans had just been discharged from the service and now wanted to become doctors, so the competition was fierce. Everett would need to get very good grades.

Everett bought a bicycle and would ride it back and forth to school most of the year. One day, in his junior year, he and I went to be interviewed by the dean of a medical school to which Everett was applying, and he rode me to the appointment on his bicycle.

As we approached the appointed place, a stranger was standing outside the building. We went on in, and the man followed us and introduced himself as Dean Clark, from The College of Medical Evangelists. Now we both wondered what was going on in his mind. We left it with the Lord.

1951-52

Everett's senior year was exciting. He would graduate from college with a degree in biology. Even more exciting, we expected that the all-important letter would come soon, and we would learn if he would be attending medical school that fall at the College of Medical Evangelists. I spent a lot of time praying about it, and I'm sure Everett did too.

Finally, the day came for our second interview with Dean Clark. This time we made sure to walk to the appointment in a dignified manner. He jokingly asked us how the bicycle was doing—all very friendly, very nice. We had no clue what he was thinking about us.

I thought of the words, "With man this is impossible, but not with God; all things are possible with God" Mark 10:27 *NIV*.

Roen and Everett in their trailer

Roen and Everett outside their trailer

With his hand on the tiller, Everett's dad sits on
the earth-moving machine that he built and that
ultimately took his life.

Chapter 10

Learning

*G*etting ready for graduation kept us busy, as we guessed who would get the acceptance letters welcoming the pre-med students into medical school. As time grew shorter, we frequented the post office, watching for that coveted letter from the medical school. One day Everett phoned me at work and said that he had the letter in his hand, but that he wouldn't open it until I got home. I couldn't wait. When we finally opened it, our hearts jumped with joy. Our dreams were coming true. He had been accepted!

Everett's mother decided to stay in College Place while he was at medical school in Loma Linda, California. She had made friends in the Walla Walla Valley and had enough work. So we decided to move in June, as I thought it would be easier to find a job before everyone else arrived and started looking. It worked out well. I took a résumé to Norton Air Force Base, with some letters of recommendation, and was hired right away, at the same pay rate I had just left.

Then we had to decide where to live. I did not want to move our trailer down and live in it again. I told Everett I thought we could do better, so I contacted the University to see if any veterans' housing was available. They wrote back that there was a one-room apartment that we could rent for what turned out to be about the same amount of money as we had been paying to park our trailer each month. This was good news! After what we had been living in, the one-room apartment sounded huge to me. There was a kitchen in one end of the room and a bathroom with a shower indoors. How exciting!

So we set out to sell our trailer. We'd lived in it for three and a half years, and that was enough. We'd paid $2,800 for it, paid rent to park it, and now were selling it for $700—so we hadn't saved much money by living in it all that time. In any case, we were moving on.

We were both happy that Everett was going to medical school, but somehow I was even more ecstatic about the idea of having a bathroom in our apartment! We had prayed for this day, and now we were on our way. We thanked the Lord for working out His will in our lives and told Him that we highly approved of the way He was doing it.

———

To make the move we bought an old, two-wheeled utility trailer for $25 and loaded all our personal belongings into it. This included a refrigerator we'd purchased for $50. There was no room in the car for any luggage or household goods, since Everett's mother and two sisters had asked to ride the 240 miles to Portland with us.

We had accumulated a surprising amount of belongings in less than four years, and now the trailer was loaded to overflowing. At last we threw a tarp over it and prayed that it would hold up for the trip. We were driving a 1946 DeSoto, and when we were about 35 miles from Portland, we began to hear a terrible scraping noise coming from the trailer, and Everett could feel the wheel pulling. He stopped the car and jumped out, looked the situation over, and decided that he would have to drive ahead to buy parts in Portland.

His mother and sisters wanted to go parts-hunting with him, so I was elected to stay and guard the trailer. We put his mother and sisters' suitcases into the car, unhooked the trailer, and away they went. Fortunately the weather was dry, but cloudy.

I stood for a while, then grew weary and sat down on the ground, leaning against a trailer tire. Time went by slowly, and I began to get sleepy. After an hour or so, I moved so I could see the traffic coming from Portland, since I felt Everett should be showing up soon. All of a sudden I heard a semi-truck braking to a stop near me. It startled me, and I offered up a quick prayer for safety. The driver got out and walked toward me. "Are you all right?" he asked. I assured him that I was, and that I expected my husband to drive up any minute. He said, "Well, a man just jumped out in front of my truck, and it looked like he was trying to commit suicide. So when I saw you hunched up against the trailer, I thought maybe he had killed you." That really got my attention. I assured him that I was all right and thanked him for stopping to check on me. After he pulled away, all sleepiness was gone, though it was beginning to get dark. So I sat on the ground beside the tire, trying to stay out of sight.

Several hours later I was still sitting there, cold, hungry, scared, and wondering what was taking Everett so long. I tried to imagine what I would do if he didn't come back, when all of a sudden he pulled up beside the trailer. I said a prayer of thanksgiving. He told me that since the trailer was built on the rear-end chassis of an old "Moon" car, he'd been unable to find any parts for it. So he had contacted some friends, and they'd said that if he could manage to get the trailer to their place, we could unload our things in their garage and fix the trailer there.

Everett thought we should try to pull the trailer the 35 miles to their house, and I agreed. I did not want to stay with the trailer all night, so we removed some of the heavy things from the trailer and put them into the car, then hooked the trailer back up and very slowly pulled out onto the highway. Our progress was slow and noisy. Sometime after midnight we scraped our way into our friend's driveway.

Two days later we were back on the road. We decided to take the coastal route to Southern California, so we could enjoy the scenery and stop and see Everett's grandparents in Eureka. But we had only been on our way for about an hour when a wheel came off the trailer in McMinnville, Oregon, and rolled to the side of the road. No one was hurt, but there was lots of traffic, and the rogue tire could have injured someone or caused damage to another car.

In a couple of hours we were on our way again, hurrying to get to his grandparents' house. When we arrived, his grandmother offered to fix supper, and since we were tired and hungry, we agreed. I noticed that as she was peeling some fresh peaches, one of them slipped out of her hands and rolled across the floor—a wooden floor with many slivers. But she simply picked up the peach, brushed it off, and sliced it into the dish with the rest.

Then, when we sat down to eat, Grandfather proudly poured us each a tall glass of warm milk, fresh from a goat. I had never tasted goat's milk before, and it bothered me that I could see little black specks floating around in it. I tasted it, and then held my breath and gulped the whole glass full down quickly, because otherwise I didn't think I could stand it. Grandpa immediately jumped up and refilled my glass, and I looked at Everett and he looked at me and whispered that I didn't have to drink it, and I noticed that he had barely touched his milk.

They invited us to stay overnight, but we said we needed to be on our way. We drove on to a campsite in the Redwoods and warmed up a can of tomato soup to take the taste of goats milk out of our mouths. We camped there that night and were on our way early the next morning. The trip went well, as we looked forward to moving into our new living quarters.

The apartment had a closet that we could actually stand in, but the closet had no door. The closet wall faced the living room, and I decided to feature it, so I bought some wallpaper with ivy climbing up a trellis and pasted it on the wall. I was so proud of the effect, but by the next day it had all peeled off. So I knew I had a lot to learn about wallpapering.

The apartment had a built-in bookcase that divided the eating area from the sleeping area. We fashioned a desk beside it for Everett and joked about me knowing the back of his head better than his face, because I would be seeing a lot more of it.

One day I cooked some navy beans in the pressure cooker on the stove next to the bookcase. That day I learned another lesson: It's not good to cook beans in a pressure cooker. Before I knew it, the beans had plugged up the vent hole and blown the weight up to the ceiling, along with a lot of bean soup! When it all started dripping back down, it coated a number of the books in the bookcase.

One of the first big, exciting classes Everett took was anatomy. Anatomy lab required the students to wear white gowns while working on the cadavers. We didn't have money to buy two of these gowns, so I took two white cotton sheets we'd received as wedding gifts, drew a pattern, and sewed the sheets into gowns. We didn't want to spend the money to have them laundered, so I took care of that too. This worked fine until I went to iron them. Only then did I discover that the cadavers' preservative solution had not been entirely washed away—in fact, it was impossible to remove it entirely by washing. And with the steam from the iron, the wretched smell wafted to my nose, gagging me with the nauseating stench. I calmed myself, *"This is the way it is, just be thankful this is not costing you anything."* I gagged every time I ironed the gowns, all year.

Everett told me that it would save us a lot of money if I could ride a bicycle back and forth to work, and I agreed that it would sure beat walking the three miles each way. So he found me an old balloon-tire bike for $15 and proudly brought it home to me. The exercise would be good for me, I thought, though it was summertime when we got the bike, and the days were getting hot.

After work one day, I was pumping as hard as I could to get home as fast as I could, to do some housework. All of a sudden I felt really flushed and weak, so I stopped, got off the bicycle, and sat down on someone's lawn. As I was sitting there, I began to think I might be having a heat stroke. After resting for some time, I got back on my bike and slowly pedaled home. When Everett arrived, I told him about my feeling weak on the ride home, and he told me I must ride slowly when it is hot—to just slow down. Another lesson learned. Once in a great while he would pick me up in the car, when the Loma Linda heat grew unbearable.

But my joust with the elements was not yet over. One drizzly morning, I put on a "slicker," or raincoat, before biking to work. On the way I hit a bump in the road, fell off the bike, and both the bike and I went scooting across the road on my "slicker," right in front of a whole string of cars. Fortunately, the cars were able to stop without hitting me, but it scared me, and I wracked my brain to try to figure out how to prevent something like this happening again. I would just have to be more careful! I looked forward to the day when I wouldn't have to ride my bicycle to work anymore. *Maybe later!*

I worked in the cost-accounting department at Norton Air Force Base, where they had just installed a huge computer. Bookkeeping machines were being replaced. One day, a co-worker twice my age took me off to the side. She said, "Roen, you are making us all look bad. You have got to quit working so hard. It won't do you any good. You won't make any more money, you won't get anywhere, and it just makes the rest of us look bad."

I could not believe that an adult professional was saying this to me. I had always believed that a responsible person accomplished as much work as possible. So I paid no attention to what she'd said and kept on doing the best I could. I'd started with a GS-1 pay scale rating and had worked up to a GS-5. Each time I'd advance, I'd get a raise. The GS-5 was about as high as I could go at that time.

There were many orange groves in and around Loma Linda back then, and in the wintertime the owners would fire up smudge pots in the groves to keep the fruit trees from freezing. These pots each held several gallons of coal oil, and when they were burning they created a lot of black smoke that warmed the air around the trees. That first fall and winter in Loma Linda were cold, and on my first morning after riding my bicycle through the black smoke, people laughed at me when I arrived at work. So I checked myself out in the mirror and saw that my face was black, especially around my nose and mouth. Now I understood.

1953

Thanksgiving time was near, and some dear friends who were studying on the Los Angeles campus of the medical school, invited us to spend it with them. After we arrived, they suggested that we all go watch the filming of the television program, Jack Bailey's "Queen for a Day." They explained that they had tried, and failed, to get tickets; however, we could go stand in the "no ticket line." They invited another couple to come along, and we all left early so we could be near the front of the line.

Eventually some ushers came by and gave each of the men a card on which to write a wish—since once a year the program crowned a "King for a Day." Before long the ushers opened the doors and let us into the auditorium.

We were having a great time visiting with our friends, when suddenly we realized that Everett's name was being called over the public address system to come onstage. We were amazed! Everett was wearing a blue plaid shirt, and a sport coat, both of which I had made, and some slacks in so-so condition. His shoes both had holes in the soles. While he was sitting onstage with the cameras on him, he nervously crossed one of his feet over a knee, and the hole was clearly much bigger than I had realized!

The Emcee had called three other men to sit onstage with Everett, and he read off the wishes each had made. Everett had written that he wanted to get an amateur radio transmitter for his former classmate Al, who had been in an accident while fighting a forest fire the previous summer. Everett and I taught a free class in amateur radio at the college, and Al was one of our students. The top of a burning tree had fallen on him, paralyzing him from his waist down, and he was receiving a lot of therapy. We reasoned that it would help him relieve boredom and deal with the grief, if he could talk as well as listen to others around the world. His classmates had given him a fine amateur radio receiver, but he still needed a transmitter.

The applause meter peaked when Everett's wish was read, and he became "King for a Day!" We were beside ourselves with joy, knowing that Al would be thrilled. But then the announcer began reading off a list of gifts that Everett and I would receive. This came as a total shock, since we had never watched the program and didn't know about the other gifts the winner received. That day we received sweaters, hats, a tuxedo, a suede jacket, and yes, two pairs of shoes for Everett. For me there was a Rose Marie Reed swimming suit, a nice raincoat, and a dozen pairs of nylons. We also received a chest-style freezer and an RCA television. Though color TV was still a thing of the future, our black-and-white TV made us the envy of Everett's classmates. All of a sudden our one-room apartment became an extremely popular place to visit (good thing we weren't still living in the trailer!). We also got a chauffeured trip to Death Valley, and since neither of us had ever before stayed in a hotel, we felt elegant. Everything was provided for us, including food, a tour of the castle, and a visit with Death Valley Scotty.

For the first two years of medical school, we remained in Loma Linda, but for the last two we had to move to Los Angeles, where the students got clinical training at the White Memorial and Los Angeles County hospitals. That meant that I had to look for a new job. Early on I made out several résumés and took them to Los Angeles. I reasoned that I would probably do best if I stayed in government employ, since that was where I had most of my experience.

I took a day off to go job-hunting with Everett, but every place I went, the answer was, "Sorry, we are having a 'reduction in force.'" I was getting a bit discouraged, so I told Everett that I had one more résumé and wanted to take it to the Corps of Engineers. I breathed a prayer, asked Everett to drive around the block while I went inside, and told him that I would be right out. I went directly to the personnel department and asked if any jobs were available. The clerk told me that they were having a "reduction in force" and weren't hiring at the time. I replied, "I used to work for the Corps of Engineers at Walla Walla, Washington, and wondered if perhaps I had some skills that you need here."

She broke into a smile and asked, "Do you know Harry Berger?" I replied, "Yes, I know him; he was head of personnel in Walla Walla when I worked there, and he and my boss were golfing buddies." She said, "Oh, just a minute!"

Soon she came back with Harry Berger. With a big smile he said, "Roen, good to see you! If you want a job, you can start Monday?" I said, "Yes, I would love to have a job, but I can't start Monday, because I have to give two weeks notice to my present employer—how would that be?"

I gave my notice and made arrangements to stay with friends in Los Angeles until Everett finished the school year there and could join me. We were close friends with some of the medical students in the class ahead of us. They graciously invited me to stay with them for the month till school was out.

Harry Berger knew me because of the extraordinary amount of overtime I'd put in at Walla Walla. I'd worked in various offices under him, where they'd often ask for me by name. Now I was able to start at the same pay rate I had been getting in Loma Linda.

Another answered prayer!

As I was discussing these matters with Harry Berger, Everett was on Figueroa Street, circling the block time after time and about to run out of gas. But when I came out of the building, with a big smile on my face, all was forgiven. We had a wonderful time of thanksgiving.

Everett served as a surgical technician in the army during World War II, and he'd learned to enjoy medical work. But no one in his family had every gone to college before, so I thought it was wonderful that he had the ambition to work and study hard. Most men in his family either worked in the woods or did odd jobs—they seemed content just to get by from day to day. They'd tried to get their children to finish grade school, maybe high school. But none were avid readers or high achievers.

Part of Everett's incentive came from the financial assistance he would receive as a veteran and his mother's encouragement. He had been in the service less than 18 months, so he didn't receive a lot of benefits, but what he did receive helped a great deal. I constantly encouraged him, as well, and told him that I knew he could do it with the Lord's help, and that I was praying for him.

In my family, my mother always wanted a college education, but it took her a long time to get one. She finally graduated with a degree in education, cum laude, in 1954, a year before Everett graduated from medical school. I was proud of her for living up to her dreams.

I always knew that I could count on Everett's complete faithfulness as a husband. But while he was in college, a neighbor told me that I was crazy to work so hard to help him get through medical school, because he would probably just leave me after he graduated. I said, "You don't know my husband, he would never leave me, he is totally faithful to me." I had faith in him and faith in the Lord.

My biggest dream was to have a family. I couldn't wait to have children that I could shower with love and acceptance. Everett kept saying, "No, we can't have a family until we are out of medical school." But most of the other medical students were having children, and I wanted us to know that joy. The Lord would provide.

I helped give a lot of showers for others who were expecting babies, and I made good friends with some of our colleagues' children. But I longed to hold our own baby in my arms. I just knew that when I had a baby, I would never-ever push it away from me, hit it, or be mean to it, as my mother had done to me. *Maybe later!*

I had very little contact with my mother after I married. The summer after Everett's sophomore year in medical school, he rode with a fellow medical student to pick up a new 1953 Dodge we could buy in Kentucky for a good price. Everett wanted to stop at my parents' place in Tennessee to see them, on his way through, and then go pick up the car. I'd written to my parents and told them he was coming and that I would be flying back to meet him, and that we would then drive home together.

When my mother opened the door and saw Everett, she said, "What can I do for you?"

Everett replied, "Didn't you get Roen's letter?"

She said, "No, how do you know Roen?" He was floored and didn't know what to do so far away from home. But Mother walked on out to the mailbox, and there was my letter. So she invited Everett in, but he was very uncomfortable and cut the visit short.

He picked up the car in Kentucky and made it to the airport in time to meet me there. We then drove back to Mother's place in Tennessee. Neither she nor her husband showed any interest in our lives, but they were cordial. *Maybe someday!*

It was my first time ever to drive across the country. We took turns driving and sleeping and drove straight through. Staying awake was hard for me, so I would play geography games with myself, trying to picture the map of the country and figured out what city or state we would come to next.

In Texas we took the car to a Dodge dealership for a required check-up. When we opened the car door and stepped out, we were met by a wall of heat! By 9 a.m., it was 100 degrees. They told us the check-up would take two hours, so we decided to go eat a long breakfast at an air-conditioned restaurant. We had planned to go to a grocery store and buy a few things to munch on, but it was far too hot to remain that long in a place without air conditioning . We were glad to pick up the car on schedule and be on our way.

We made it home, exhausted, grimy, and thankful for God's care and protection. The only stop of any length had been at the dealer's, and we were pleased that we had not had to spend any money on sleeping accommodations. Thinking back, we were a little presumptuous to ask God to keep us safe under those circumstances.

1954

Everett signed up with others in his class to take a six-week tropical medicine course in Mexico during the summer, and I arranged to take four weeks of annual leave to join him. Bill, one of Everett's unmarried classmates; his classmate Al; and Al's wife, Fern, arranged to ride down with Everett in our new car; I flew down and met them later in Veracruz. My flight was rough, and I was neither a frequent flyer nor a brave one. I spent a lot of time praying. A lady behind me had several children strapped into two seats, vomiting and out of control, and the captain informed us that we would have to make an emergency landing at a small airport to clean the plane.

How happy and thankful I was to rush into Everett's arms at

Veracruz. I had taken—and enjoyed—two years of Spanish in high school, and it came in handy now, as I volunteered to help with the shopping and cooking. I enjoyed bargaining with the vendors at the market. They were patient with my limited Spanish, and sometimes they would laugh with me about it. So many sights, sounds, and smells were new to me.

The next part of Everett's program took us to Mexico City. We stayed there for a few days and then headed back up the coast toward home.

At Mazatlán, there was no bridge to join the southern part of the town to its northern part, so we had to go on a "ferry," which consisted of two row boats, side by side, with planks laid across them and fastened to the outer sides. The boatmen pulled the ferry up to the ramp and told Everett to drive the car on and that they would take us passengers in a rowboat. When I saw my husband and our nearly new car going across the river on that thing, I prayed hard. The boatmen pushed long poles down into the shallow water to move the ferry forward. We all arrived safely on the other side, and even today when I see beautiful pictures of Mazatlán, all I see in my mind is that little "ferry" out on the water with my husband and our new car, and two smiling men propelling it with poles.

We were humbled by the promise, "For He shall give His angels charge over thee, to keep thee in all thy ways" Psalm 91:11, *KJV*.

Our one room apartment at Loma Linda

Chapter 11

Hanging On

1954-55

*I*t had been a nice change of pace, but now it was back to studies in the States. Everett's schedule was rather irregular those last two years of medicine, as he rotated among various departments.

We rented a flat in Boyle Heights, near the White Memorial Hospital, where he did most of his work. It was only a two-block walk to the streetcar, and I could take that streetcar to the front door of the office where I worked. If there were seats left on the streetcar, I would sit down, pull out my knitting needles and yarn, and work away on blankets and sweaters for my hoped-for baby.

Ours was a neighborhood known for some violence, and it looked rundown, so we were happy to be able to live in an upstairs flat. It had a bedroom, kitchen, bathroom, and a living room, with a foldaway bed built into the wall. I loved having more room and some privacy. But I did not enjoy sharing it with an endless stream of poison-resistant, unwelcome cockroaches.

Everett especially enjoyed the clinical part of his training. It seemed to me that he spent most of his time at the hospital, depending on what rotation he was in. Obstetrics at the County Hospital was a big one. In the six weeks he served on that rotation, he delivered 126 babies. He enjoyed it, but wondered why so many of those little ones insisted on arriving in the middle of the night.

My life, as usual, was consumed with work, church, and dreaming about having a family. I continued to help with baby showers and spend time with our friends' little ones.

Everett was dreadfully busy and constantly under mental pressure. I knew I must be pleasant and help him. Inevitably he would insist on wanting to know what I was thinking, and when I mentioned children, he would patiently explain our circumstances. But as time passed and we reached five-and-a-half years of marriage, he finally admitted that perhaps we could manage somehow to start our family. Even then I wondered if he really wanted a family, or was just trying to please me.

But month after month the stork refused to fill our order. We prayed about it and read everything we could find on infertility, and even consulted a physician, but still my hopes were dashed. I had some surgery, ate wheat germ and molasses, got lots of rest, and tried about everything anyone suggested.

One day someone asked me if I knew that my closest friend was expecting her second child. I was crushed. Why hadn't she told me? Then I figured out that she knew my longing and knew it would hurt. Everett was sympathetic but always pleaded with me to be patient. *It must be God's way.*

One evening at supper Everett told me that he had heard an excellent lecture on infertility and sterility that day, given by a physician who limited his practice entirely to such problems. Everett suggested that I make an appointment to see him. The next day I asked this doctor's nurse if they had any appointments open soon. It was with mixed feelings of apprehension that we made our first visit. As he talked with us, I was alternately scared and disgusted, happy and hopeful. He asked why we wanted a baby! Why does anybody want a family?

He did some examinations and tests and gave me a list of further tests and instructions to be followed. I learned to trust him in subsequent visits, and he gave me some hope. I'd never considered myself overweight, but he suggested that it might be advantageous for me to take off 20 pounds. But after a few visits, I meekly suggested that perhaps after all we should adopt a baby. The doctor acted insulted and scolded me; any further suggestions along those lines I kept to myself.

I carefully followed each of his orders, diets, and instructions, and after many months we began to suspect that our prayers were being answered. I visited the doctor, and he confirmed that if all went well, we should have our baby in about eight months. My joy knew no bounds! The next day I passed out candy to the entire office staff in honor of the occasion. I was going to have a baby! Maybe the celebration was a bit unusual, but the candy was good—pale pink, green, and yellow mints.

Everett's rejoicing was more muted. The custom in his class was to hand out candy bars upon the arrival of a baby among the students. But we would all be long separated by the time our baby arrived, so at the next class function, he took several sacks of little candy bars and threw them out into the group of medical students.

Meanwhile, I got busy and made several maternity outfits that I couldn't wait to wear. But to my horror, a few weeks later at work, I began to hemorrhage. I panicked and called the doctor. He asked me to come into the office. After examining me, he gave me a prescription that he said I would need to take consistently until the baby was born, but that he thought I would be all right. I asked him if it would be a good idea for me to quit my job. He said, "Absolutely not, if it is a good baby you will keep it, and if not, you don't want it anyway!" It sounded so harsh. *Of course my baby was a good baby!*

1955

Time flew by as Everett took his final tests, I finished my final days of work, and we prepared to move. Friends and family came to his graduation, and I felt so proud of him. I knew he could do it. I slipped into my new, navy blue, pleated maternity outfit—I wanted the world to know about this answered prayer! The graduation was held outside on the lawn, and Everett looked impressive in his cap, gown, and hood. Mother Wilson and the girls sat beside me, all of us smiling from ear to ear as he walked up the aisle.

Everett passed his boards, so he could practice in Oregon, and he arranged to take an internship at the Portland Adventist Sanitarium. The hospital owned some adjacent cottages for interns; each had a bedroom, a living room, a kitchen, and a bathroom—the best living accommodations we'd ever enjoyed.

We also found that we enjoyed living so near the other interns and their families, all of whom were our classmates from Loma Linda. Everett's pay was $123 a month, plus housing.

I was ironing one day when I suddenly felt a rush of water and found myself standing in a puddle. I quickly called Everett, and he told me to come on down to the hospital, only about 100 feet away. He met me at the door of the OB department and told me to wait there, as he rushed off to register me.

The long, silent hall seemed like a little bit of heaven—the beginning of the fulfillment of many dreams and prayers, as I stood there alone on the maternity wing. Presently the ward clerk approached and asked what she could do for me. Somewhat surprised, I explained that I was about to have my baby, that I would like to go to bed, and that my husband, Dr. Wilson, had gone to register me and would be right back. She looked at me in a very skeptical way and asked if I had any pain. I said yes, I was having pain right then. She looked even more skeptical and told me to just wait there for a while and the nurse would be right back. I felt resentment at her indifference, but then again, how would she know that this wasn't just another baby—that each pain was lightened by the sheer joy that soon our baby would be in my arms.

Shortly, the nurse arrived and helped me into bed, and soon Everett came back, grinning from head to toe. The labor was short, and before we knew it, they were wheeling me into the delivery room. My heart was full of praise. As they were putting my feet into the stirrups, Everett introduced me to the crew and anyone who'd dropped by. It felt like a big party. Our son, Duane, weighed in at 6 lbs., 9-1/2 ounces. He was whole and healthy—clearly the most beautiful creation I had ever seen, just the right size to fit in one of the little sweater and cap sets I'd knitted for him. It was November, snow had come early, and it looked like a fairyland outside.

I found a job doing billing and insurance forms for some anesthesiologists, working at home so I wouldn't have to leave my baby, and I continued with this job throughout Everett's one-year internship. As he was pondering where to practice, he said he wanted to take a residency in anesthesia. I didn't want to leave my baby, so I encouraged him to work for a while first.

Then my uncle came to see us and urged me to encourage Everett to go ahead and finish his training. Uncle Wells said that if Everett took his residency there in Portland, that we could stay in an apartment that my aunt and he owned above their doughnut shop. They would not charge us rent or utilities, he promised, and would even have hook-ups for a washer and dryer installed for us. What could I say! I kept right on working for the anesthesiologists, and we moved into Uncle Wells' apartment. The University only paid Everett $80 a month during his residency, but he still worked lots of hours. The residency would last two years.

1956

Baby Daryl arrived one year, one month, one week, and one day after Duane. My joy knew no bounds. A wide staircase led up to our apartment, and we had to park a little distance from where we lived, but I didn't mind the inconvenience. There was a market a few blocks from where we lived, and I'd put the boys in the stroller and we'd do our grocery shopping.

Plants have a special fascination for me, so I planted a terrarium in a 14-inch fishbowl. I was proud of my little garden. When patients called, I made a point of sounding very professional, as though I was working in a regular office. One day I was explaining to someone about insurance coverage, when Duane decided to explore the fishbowl, grabbed it, and turned it upside down over his head. He was soon sputtering, and I was doing my best not to break into peels of laughter. I politely excused myself from the phone conversation as quickly as possible and cleaned up my baby boy. The boys both walked and talked early and were very active.

Everett and I felt blessed to have had nine years together, and we knew that the grace of God had brought us this far. "O taste and see that the Lord is good; blessed is the man that trusteth in Him Psalm 34:8 *KJV*.

Everett's graduation from medical school

I pose with Everett at his graduation from Loma Linda University in 1955, wearing the maternity outfit I had lovingly made for the occasion.

My Forever Friend

Happiness to Heartaches

Book 2

Chapter 12

And Then There Were Five

oward the end of Everett's residency, I began watching newspaper ads, looking for a new family home. I noticed one advertised very near the hospital where Everett planned to practice. The owners were going on an extended trip and wanted someone to housesit. I phoned and made an appointment to check it out. It turned out to be a beautiful English Cotswold home—brick painted white, with a blue, slate roof. I fell in love with it. We entered on the bedroom floor. One step up took us to the bedrooms and bathroom, and 15 steps down took us to the living room, kitchen, dining room, den, sun porch, and sewing room. More steps took us down to the basement.

The Brewers, a gracious older couple, wanted to tour the world, and we assured them that we would take good care of their home for them while they were away. Then they mentioned that they really wanted to sell, because they would eventually be moving to California. They were willing to accept $1,000 down and $300 a month.

Everett almost panicked. He had been saying all along that he would never go into debt. He remembered how his grandfather's wheat crop had been hailed out two years in a row in Colorado, and how grandfather had fallen into debt when he had to borrow seed money. No, Everett did not want to get caught like that.

I tried to explain what a wonderful opportunity this was—that it would take years for us to save enough money to pay cash for a home of our own. Besides, I explained, it would save on income taxes if we were buying, rather than renting, a house.

The anesthesiologists I was working for had asked him to join them in their practice in Portland, where he had interned, and they assured him that his income would be adequate. I talked to God about it, as well as Uncle Wells—both of whom Everett respected highly! He was convinced! So we moved right to the house and loved living there. One side of the property bordered Mt. Tabor

Park, which had tennis courts. The south side looked out over our sunken garden and a city reservoir. What peace and beauty!

The charming house had been built in 1928 and showed excellent workmanship and care. We were excited and thankful to our Heavenly Father for providing in such a wonderful way. We didn't mind that at first we had to use boxes for bedside stands and folding chairs for living room furniture. The hardwood floors were beautiful; we didn't mind that we didn't yet have rugs for them.

1958

While the boys were napping one day, I ran down to the basement to change the washer and fold the clothes. When I came back upstairs, past the living room, I saw shards of glass spread out across the shiny hardwood living room floor. I ran to investigate and saw a stick that someone had used to break the glass and open the door. I fairly flew up the stairs to see if my boys were safe. They were both still sound asleep. But one of their banks was gone—a fairly big, heavy one in the shape of a house that contained a lot of money now, since we'd been saving since they were born.

My first thought was, *"I wonder if someone is still in the house."* But I could find no one, though I searched frantically under beds and in closets. I called the police and told them my plight. Calmly the dispatcher informed me that someone would be there in one or two hours to make a report. I cried out, "Oh, please, can't you come sooner; our lives may be in danger!" The curt reply came, "No, Lady, we are changing shifts!" *Click.*

I hung up in disbelief. Now who could I call for comfort, if not security? I didn't know any neighbors yet, and I felt alone and scared. So I fell on my knees and poured out my heart and concerns to my Heavenly Father. Then I began to feel peace. I tried to call Everett, but he was in surgery, so I left a message for him.

When the police arrived an hour and a half later, I showed them the damage and mentioned that I hoped that whoever had come in wouldn't be back. The officer looked at me with a little smile, as he examined our almost empty house. He said, *"Don't worry, Lady, they won't come back here."* And he was right!

My days were filled with joy, caring for and loving my two little boys and keeping house. The yard had been beautifully landscaped, with lots of well-established plants and shrubs. Everett worked long hours at the hospital, and he had never had the experience of learning how to care for a beautiful yard. So he showed little interest in it, and the boys and I spent a lot of happy hours working there. It took a lot more time to care for a big house than for a little apartment, but I didn't mind one bit.

Five anesthesiologists worked in Everett's group. Each would work for four weeks straight, then take a week off. It sounded like a good arrangement for them, but somehow I could never manage to have a vacation every fifth week. Everett didn't understand this; he wanted to go places and have fun with the family on his vacation weeks, and he clearly didn't want to stay home and do yard work, take care of kids, clean house, buy groceries, and do all the other things that were taking my time.

It took a whole lot of study and prayer for me to figure all this out. Everett took an interest in doing things with the boys, particularly working on cars and mechanical devices. He loved the boys, but never really thought much about what it took to keep things going at home.

1959

Diane joined our happy family when Daryl was just two. Until the day she was born, I assured everyone that having another boy would be wonderful. When a girl arrived, however, my joy knew no bounds. Now I had a baby girl! She had big, brown eyes like her Daddy's. Her brothers were full of awe and very helpful.

I loved teaching them to pray, and I read Bible stories to them each day. We went to church every week and enjoyed the spiritual blessings of our church family. If Everett was busy at the hospital, I would get the children ready for church, and off we would go by ourselves. Taking care of three little ones, three years old and under, was a challenge, but God always seemed to help me. I'd remember how my mother had pushed me away, and I'd draw my children even closer toward me. The boys loved going to the children's classes, and Diane and I joined them there. We sang songs about Jesus all week at home.

Diane started walking at nine months, and by the time she turned two, insisted on helping me vacuum the stairs. We had a Karastan carpet on them, and with Diane's help it took twice as long. But I encouraged her, and she stuck right with the job. I guess she got her fill of it, though, because now that she is grown, vacuuming the house is no longer one of her favorite pastimes.

1963

When Diane was almost four, she and the boys were all at my side one day when the phone rang: "What did you say?" I asked. "Yes, I remember the twin babies you used to care for. What? They need a home? What kind of a home, do you mean forever? Oh, yes, I will be glad to help you find a home for them."

"Who was that, Mommy?" asked seven-year-old Duane.

"Oh, it was a friend of Mommy's; she wants me to help her find a home for some twins."

"Are they going to live with us, Mommy?"

What a startling question from six-year-old Daryl! "Oh, please, Mommy, are they girls? You know how I have been praying for a sister," said Diane.

Four-year-old Diane had been praying for a sister, but this was a girl and a boy, already a year old! "Well," I said, "we will talk to Daddy about it."

The conversation that day was mostly about babies, where they would sleep, when we would get them, what they would look like, and who would get to dress them. The idea of adopting them tumbled around in my mind, and my feelings ranged from sheer terror to eager anticipation. Hadn't Diane been praying for a sister? Was this an answer to prayer? The boy would be a bonus. I had always wanted a large family to love and enjoy, but two more children? Could we do them justice? My friend Darlene had said that the children were both ill and needed medical attention—that they had lived in five different homes already! *How sick were they?*

Late in the day when Daddy called home, I casually asked him how he would like to adopt twins. There was a long silence. Then in slow, measured words, he quietly said, "I won't say no, let's think about it." Meanwhile, enthusiasm was mounting on the home front, and since the babies needed a home now, we arranged to visit them, to see if we thought they just might fit in.

They were indeed in poor health, running high fevers and looking listless, without the skills most one-year-olds display. They immediately accepted us and our tender, caressing words. I thought of my own childhood of rejection and wanted to take them home that minute and show them what a loving, caring home was like. Daddy wasn't quite so sure. He suggested that we have them evaluated medically.

The tests were not completely satisfactory. The doctor suggested that we take them for a year, and if everything looked favorable, to go ahead and adopt them. When we got home with the twins, the boys had already stacked their bunk beds so there would be room for David's crib, and Diane had all her special toys laid out for Debbi.

David continued to have a high temperature; Debbi's soon dropped to normal. She would crawl around from one to another, climb up on our laps, then slide off and go to someone else. We took the twins to see a pediatrician, and he ordered medicine for their coughs and fever. They improved slowly, but steadily. David just wanted to sit on my lap and hang onto me. He would go sound asleep, his little hands holding onto my clothes so tightly that I could hardly pry them loose.

As their health improved, however, we knew we couldn't hold out a year to adopt them, and we began saying, "Maybe this will be your sister and brother!" In three short months they were ours, as the judge said, "Forever and ever."

The children were 14 months old when they arrived at our home. Debbi could crawl, but not David, whose motor skills were underdeveloped. I concentrated on giving them the best possible food for their age and making sure they got lots of sleep and lots of love. Debbi had a habit of folding her hands together and sucking both thumbs at the same time. She'd suck so hard, she got big blisters on both thumbs.

I made little red coats and hats for the twins, and red velveteen outfits, too. Sewing for all of the children was a joy. When Daryl and Duane were eight and nine, they wanted to learn to sew, so I helped each of them make a shirt. They were proud of those shirts and wore them to shreds.

As the twins got stronger, they began learning and doing things typical of other children their age. Debbi started walking at 18 months and David finally did so at age two. They were soon joining in our songs and loved going to Sabbath school. When they were two and a half, I taught the twins to sing *Timothy Was a Very Good Boy*, in harmony. They presented it for church, and right in the middle, they traded soprano and alto parts. I was amazed. I had had to pick the parts out on the piano to teach them.

David and Debbi both loved to climb up on the piano bench and play the piano. I taught them to play *Jesus Loves Me* with one finger, and, of course, *Chopsticks*. They picked up on it so fast, Everett said, "I want you to find them the best teacher you can. They have talent." I wondered if David would have a problem because of his slow motor movements, but I determined to find the best.

Sometimes I wondered if life could possibly be happier than this. "Sing unto Him, sing psalms unto Him, talk ye of all His wondrous works. Glory ye in His holy name; let the heart of them rejoice that seek the Lord" 1 Chronicles 16:9-10 *KJV*.

Chapter 13

Resolution

1968

$\mathcal{T}$he shrill ring of the telephone broke the stillness of the night. My cousin in Tennessee was on the line, calling to tell me that my parents had been in a tragic accident in South Georgia. Ervin, my stepfather, had been killed, and my mother had a head injury and a broken shoulder and ribs. While driving their pickup on the freeway, they had been hit on the left rear fender, and their vehicle had gone end-over-end three times down the highway. Ervin's head had been crushed between the pavement and the car. Mother had a huge bruise across her lap, from the tension of the seatbelt.

He gave me the hospital's phone number, and I quickly called for more information. The nurse told me that Mother was in and out of consciousness and was being medicated for pain. I asked the nurse to tell Mother that I would be there as soon as I could arrange for a babysitter and get plane reservations.

I asked my Best Friend to come close to Mother, to help me figure everything out, and to help me be a blessing to her in her time of need. Jesus had never let me down, and I knew that He was my strength in time of trouble.

Everett's mother readily agreed to stay with the children while I was away, and suggested that she ask her sister and brother-in-law, Vyda and Ray, to come and stay for a while. I had no idea how long I would be gone, and Everett could not take time out from his practice. I was able to fly out that very day, after a whirlwind of preparation. My mind flitted from one scenario to another. I wanted so much to be of help to Mother, to tell her that I forgave her, to give her some hope. But did she want to be forgiven? Did she even realize how hard she had made my life?

When I arrived, I gathered my luggage and took a taxi to the hospital. As I tiptoed into Mother's room, she opened her eyes a little, and a smile started to spread over her face. "You came," she said simply.

I gave her a hug and kiss and asked a few questions about where she hurt and how she felt. Her voice was weak and faraway, and I didn't want to tire her, so at first I just stood by her bed, my hand touching her. When I prayed out loud for her, I could feel her relax.

When she drifted off to sleep, I went to a public payphone to make some calls.

I had never been in that part of the country before and wasn't used to the local way of speaking. Most of my calls were operator assisted, and finally the poor operator said, "I'm sorry, Honey, but I just can't understand you!" I assured her that I was having the same problem.

Finally the arrangements were made. The doctor assured me that Mother could be transferred to the Erlanger Hospital, in Chattanooga, Tennessee, but advised me not to expect her to be able to attend Ervin's funeral.

After contacting his four children and Cathie and Al, we decided to arrange to have the funeral on Friday at the church Mother and Ervin attended. Cathie arrived on Thursday; mother and I arrived via an ambulance plane. Since I wasn't an enthusiastic flyer, I felt each bump and wondered at each change in the sound of the engine.

Mother was improving, but agreed that she would not be able to go to the funeral. Ervin's oldest daughter, Louise, also came.

The day after the funeral, Cathie and Louise went to visit Mother and then flew home. I stayed. July can be very hot and muggy in Ooltewah, Tennessee, where Mother lived. The country was pretty, but the heat was miserable. Each day I would drive to the hospital to see Mother and spend as much time with her as I could. She begged me to stay longer and help her figure out what to do. She seemed glad to have me there, and it felt good to hear her say so.

Before the accident, she had planned to teach school again that fall. But now those plans would have to change. Her mind was simply not functioning well enough yet, and her body hurt everywhere. She begged me not to go home and leave her there alone, where she had no family. I assured her that I would stay until she could come home with me.

My days were full, because I was trying to take care of her business while packing up her things. We decided that Everett and our boys, Duane and Daryl, would fly out later and load her things into a rented truck and drive them back to Portland. When she was ready to leave the hospital, I took her home, and as her health improved, we continued making plans and arrangements. We sold the things she didn't want to move, as well as the house. Her car would be towed behind the truck.

In the middle of the night I was surprised when Mother spoke and asked if I was awake. I told her I was. She said, "I don't know how you can be so good to me when I have treated you as I have all your life." My mind raced, searching for the right words.

I didn't dare speak the forbidden words while she was sick in mind and body. I longed to take the opportunity, but knew I had to do the right thing. I finally reminded her that Jesus loves us with unconditional love, and I loved her the same way. She promptly drifted off to sleep and didn't mention it again.

Three weeks to the day after the accident, she and I were ready to fly to Portland. Everything was packed and ready. She asked to take her portable typewriter and tape recorder with her on the plane. We also took a heavy coat for her, because of the uncertain Northwest weather and her tendency to feel cold. We changed planes once. I can still vividly remember pushing her in a wheelchair in Chicago's O'Hare airport, heavily loaded with the carry-ons, almost running to make the next plane. I felt so out-of-breath.

Everett and the children were elated when we arrived, and my joy knew no bounds. Home again with my family, and my mother! Diane and Debbi willingly turned their room over to "Grandma Baker" and moved to the basement. The boys, meanwhile, were looking forward to their trip to Tennessee with Dad. School would be starting soon, so they would have to go get Grandma's things soon.

After they left, I turned my attention full time to Mother and the three younger children. We enjoyed catching up on what had happened during the past three weeks, and I tried gently to help Mother settle in. I also watched for any opportunity to have a good talk. But I could see that the door to her heart was closed for now. *Maybe later!* She said she wanted to stay with us. I told her that in that case, we would build a room onto our house, with her own bathroom in it for privacy, so the girls could have their room back. Mother was mourning the loss of her husband, with whom she said she had enjoyed 25 perfect years.

When Everett and the boys arrived with her things, we had to find a place to put them. Fortunately we had a good-sized basement and put most of it there. Everett agreed that Mother could stay on with us, and we contacted a builder and began preparing the ground to build a foundation for her room. But Mother felt her help was needed in the disciplining of our now-five-year-old twins, and David and Debbi resented her demands. So I kindly asked Mother to leave disciplinary matters to Everett and me. She flared into a rage and slammed the door as she rushed into her room. When she came out, she called my sister, Cathie, and asked her to come get her.

Cathie came that afternoon to pick Mother up and as many of her things as she could fit into the car. Mother wouldn't speak to me. They left, and I thought my heart would break once again. There went my mother. The girls were thrilled to have their room back, and our home became quiet and peaceful again. I tried to call Mother, but she wouldn't speak to me. For two years all communication was done through my sister. Through Cathie she asked to have all her things taken from our house to Cathie's, and we promptly complied.

From time to time I sent Mother a card or a note, but she never responded. Finally she began to acknowledge me a little and would say hello to me if I called my sister's house and she answered the phone. But never did she say, "I'm sorry, let's be friends." My sister helped her find a house to buy, a couple miles from where she lived, so Mother was able to be back on her own again. Several years later she asked me to take her to medical appointments, and though this complicated my life, I made it a priority to be there for her.

After Cathie married again and moved away, Mother began to call me every day at 9:00 a.m. If I was busy or couldn't visit just then, she would become upset and point out that she was my mother, and at least I could reserve that time for her.

She said that she would like to live closer to us so that I could help her get her groceries and do yard work. She did have beautiful flowers in the summertime. I helped her find a nice, little house, a couple of miles from ours. We moved her in with Tweety Bird, her canary. She didn't have enough money and not much income, so Everett agreed that we would make her house payments, and we did this for several years.

1994

Her hip began to give her a lot of pain, and her doctor said she needed a total hip operation. A week or so after the surgery, while still in the hospital, she started having a lot of pain in her stomach area and spitting up blood. The surgeon said that she needed to have part of her stomach removed. Shortly after surgery, her blood pressure dropped dangerously low, her breathing stopped, and she nearly died. She had signed a statement that she did not want to be resuscitated if it came to that, but in the frenzy of the moment, nobody noticed the order, and they brought her back from the brink.

As she was recovering in the hospital, I explained to her that I would not be able to bring her home and take care of her. We would have to find a facility where she could live. She agreed to that, for which I was thankful, because at one point she had said, "Don't you ever put me in a nursing home."

She was 89, and we found a nice nursing facility where she would have good care. I went to see her as often as I could and took her flowers and cards. One day she seemed perky and said to me, "You look so nice today, that color is lovely on you." I was almost overcome with emotion, and I replied, "Oh, thank you so much, Mother, you haven't always talked to me like that." She replied, "I know I haven't, can you ever forgive me for treating you as I have all your life?" She began crying and tearfully asked, "Can we start over from today?" Words that I had longed to hear most of my life had finally been spoken. I assured her that she was forgiven. Soon after that her mind closed down, and she could no longer recognize me or respond in any way. I thanked my Friend for those priceless moments of reconciliation. She died a few days before her 99th birthday.

I thought back to the day when I had written and asked her why she treated me differently than my sister and brother. She'd replied, "You can't expect me to treat you like I did the other children. After all, you were born at a very hard time in my life." It didn't matter anymore. I had forgiven her.

"For thou, Lord, art good, and ready to forgive; and plenteous in mercy unto all that call upon thee" Psalm 86:5 *KJV*.

Chapter 14

Enjoying Life

The twins' prodigious musical talent revealed in leaps and bounds. Early on we discovered that Deb would ask her brother, Dave, to play their new pieces first; then she would sit down and play them as if she knew exactly what she was doing. I sat with each of them as they'd practiced, and when I asked her to play a new piece first, I found that she was not learning to read music, but was playing from the tune in her head. I spoke to their music teacher about this, and from then on, she gave them different music from different books and warned them never, never to play each other's assigned music.

When he was 10, Dave decided that he wanted to learn to play the organ. I did some research and interviewed a Mr. Fawk, who taught in Salem, Oregon, about 45 miles away. We were impressed and signed both twins up for organ lessons, since by then Deb was saying that she, too, wanted to learn to play the organ. But Mr. Fawk wisely advised that it would be better for her to concentrate on becoming a really good pianist, so each of them would have their own special area of musical expertise.

It proved to be a good arrangement. Deb learned to read music and her skills progressed marvelously, and though Dave had some coordination problems, his motor skills for playing the organ were unimpaired. With Mr. Fawks' guidance, he too became proficient.

Then Mr. Fawk asked if he could take our 13-year-old son on a month-long tour in Europe, where Dave would give 32 concerts in 30 days, on pipe organs in cathedrals all over the continent. We were excited and gave our blessing. The tour brought our son into contact with the European side of classical music and we noticed, upon his return, how he had matured musically and socially.

Our home in the country sat atop a hill on 19 acres. A little creek gurgled by, 50 feet from the house. We had an orchard and a large garden plot. But the children had decided that having horses wasn't as much fun as they thought it would be. It took a lot of time and energy to care for horses, and they'd decided that dirt bikes would be more fun. On the other hand, Everett wanted them to learn about farm life, so we raised some chickens and enjoyed gathering their eggs. Everett also got three heifers to raise and sell for beef. Mandy, a Black Angus and leader of the three, specialized in breaking fences.

The pasture consisted of a fairly steep, grassy hillside that sloped down to another creek. Mandy would break out, and the others would follow her. I would then grab the twins and chase the cows into the barn until Everett got home to fix the fence. One day Mandy broke through the fence down at the very bottom of the hill, and it took us hours to get them rounded up and into the barn. By that time I was huffing and puffing and felt as if I couldn't take another breath.

So I went directly to the phone and called Everett to tell him that I had chased cows for the last time. It was just too hard to breathe, and there was no reason to put myself through that for the small amount of return they would bring. He gave me permission to sell them, and I did right away.

Everett delighted in planning outings for the kids and once took the boys and a couple of their friends on a hike for several days through the wilderness. Later he took Diane on a weekend motorcycle trip, and they both loved their one-on-one time together. Everett also planned endless day trips—water skiing, canoeing, bicycling, and hiking. When the twins were six, we took a weeklong trip around the Bowron lakes in Canada. Everett's mother and aunt joined us. We spent long, lazy days paddling across the lakes, camping by the campfire in the evening, often with other travelers. There we enjoyed swapping stories with one particular group from Canada.

The next day as we were making a fairly long portage, one of the men from Canada came upon Debbi and stopped in the middle of the trail. Her sleeping bag had fallen off her backpack and unrolled. He asked her if he could help her.

She promptly replied, "No, thank you, I can handle it myself;

my mommy taught me not to talk to strangers." It gave him quite a chuckle.

After Deb graduated from high school, she had an exciting opportunity to travel with a singing group for a year, giving Christian concerts. She would be the soprano and keyboard artist. Her voice had matured beautifully and she did a good job.

1974

Duane signed up to study in London for the summer after his senior year. He went with a group from the college he would be attending that fall, led by a friend of mine named Helen Evans. We missed him and enjoyed talking to him on the phone occasionally, especially the time he called and asked if I would fly over and travel with him for a month, after their classes were over. Other members of the class would be traveling in their own little groups.

I asked, "What young man your age would want his mother to travel with him in Europe for a month?"

He answered, "I would!"

So I just had to say "Yes!"

Everett and I talked it over, and he said he would like to join us for two weeks—which was the most time he could get off work. But he added that maybe we could pick up a car while we were there.

That sounded mighty good to me. We hadn't owned a new car since 1953, and this was 1974. We ordered a bright yellow Mercedes Benz diesel, 240D. We picked it up in Stuttgart and enjoyed touring in it for two weeks.

We roughed it, using our camping gear, and then took Everett to the airport to fly home. Duane and I then drove the car up to Bremerhaven, completed arrangements for shipping it to the United States, and boarded the ferry for England. Duane knew his way around fairly well, as he had spent a month there already. He was a great host.

I enjoyed the sights and getting acquainted with a new culture. I even decided to try out a new word I had heard, and shocked Duane one day when I said we had enjoyed "a bloody good meal."

"Mother!" he said. "I can't believe you said that!" Then he explained that I had used a swear word. I apologized and didn't try any more new words.

We included Scotland in our itinerary and both loved the time together. We camped in a smelly cow pasture and sat on the beach and watched the sun set. The rest of the time we'd stayed in a London dormitory.

We were both glad to get home and catch up on the latest with the family. The car had arrived and we all enjoyed it. Duane left for college, taking a Biophysics major with a goal of going on to medical school. I suggested that since he would need excellent grades to get into medical school, maybe he should take an easier major. He replied, "No, Mother, if I don't get into medical school, I want to be prepared to work in the field I am interested in!"

"But I rejoiced in the Lord greatly, that now at the last your care of me hath flourished again" Philippians 4:10 *KJV*.

Chapter 15

Fun for Mom and Dad

1978

*D*aryl and Diane took a year off from college to go to Indonesia and teach English and Bible, as student missionaries. I wrote the material in this chapter for them, while they were there, hoping to lighten their homesickness and give them a laugh. A few months later they returned home, and my motorcycle riding days were over.

***

There's something special about spring—even for Mom and Dad. This is especially true when Dad has a day off from the old grind, the sun is shining, and it's a bit warm outside—oh, maybe 60 degrees.

Dad sidled up to Mom with his big, knowing grin, and said, "Honey, I would like to do something special for you today. What would you like it to be?" Mom, burdened down with a multitude of things that needed her attention that very day, and thinking of a number of things that needed Dad's attention, hesitates for a moment, regains her composure, and blurts out, "Well, how would a cycle ride be?"

Instant success! Dad's smile widens, and the only decision left to be made is where to go! Several alternatives come up: The back road to the cabin—too much gravel! Kahneeta—a long-ways round trip and maybe ice! Estacada—too much traffic! George—perfect! George it will be!

We climb into our phosphorescent orange riding suits and start the scramble for gloves, helmets, boots, and so forth. Dad generously gives Mom the bright-orange Bell helmet with the visor. Mom puts it on, just about gets the strap fastened, then frantically takes it back off her head. Ah, wonderful fresh air. Sheepishly she puts the thing back on her head and fastens it up, all the while telling herself that wearing the helmet is not so bad. Everybody wears the things, it's safer—but, alas, there it comes off again!

Defeated and embarrassed, she explains to Dad that she wishes he would wear the helmet that encloses the face and she can wear one of the other helmets—not that she doesn't appreciate his taking such good care of her, but the helmet is, well, so closed in! Dad understands and sweetly goes back to the pile and picks a different helmet out and brings it to her—complete with goggles. Yes, much better; and yes, these gloves are fine.

Oh, I guess I don't have much gas in this thing. I should have thought of that. Dad volunteers to take care of the matter. But first he must take off the orange thing, find the keys to the Carryall so he can move it out of the way, and get the cycle up to the gas pump.

Oh, my boots, where are my boots? I told Dave he could wear them, but he couldn't get them on. Where could he have left them? Yes, I searched his room and they aren't there. I dig in the pile in the garage. Oh happy day, there they are under the hockey gear! What's the matter, have my feet grown? No, I just have to leave the pant legs on the outside.

Ah, we're ready to go. Wait a minute, I haven't ridden this motorcycle since I took my test. Now, how do I shift? Which way do you turn the throttle to get more gas? Where is the kill button? The horn? Oh, yes, I am beginning to remember. Dad thoughtfully suggests that perhaps it would be a good idea to ride around the yard a bit before we hit the road.

There! I am beginning to get the feel again! "I will follow you," I say. Down to the highway—no cars coming! This is wonderful! Up Firwood Road, everything is under control. I sure am glad Dad is only going about 40 mph. I venture from one gear to another and begin to feel a faint confidence.

Oh no! The corner! What if someone is coming? What if I hit gravel? What if I swing too wide? Well, it isn't so bad! Dad pulls over to the side and motions me over to see how everything is going. I give him a big smile and tell him, "Fine!" Well, that is until I let out on the clutch again.

I forget to give the bike enough gas as I take off up a bit of a hill, and it is suddenly very quiet. I push the start button, embarrassed—it's still very quiet! The battery is dead! Dad very sweetly gets off his cycle, and gets on mine. He gets it going with the kick-starter. We try again, this time with success—sort of. I don't want to kill it again, so to avoid that problem, I give it the gas and take off like a streak, spewing gravel! Fortunately I soon get it under control and we are on our way.

Dad told me about the pretty country we were going through. I am sure we were, but I have no way of knowing other than taking his word for it, because I was really busy watching the road. Funny thing, I was so good at spotting each bump. I watched carefully, and I don't believe I missed a single bump. It worked the same with the holes. Then there was the washboard! The interesting thing about that particular road was that there was a lot of variety—right in the surface of the road itself. I didn't have to look away once!

In fact, suddenly there was no more pavement—just gravel! I had some experience with gravel some years earlier on my bicycle, and I didn't forget it because it took so long to get the gravel out of my knees and heal up the holes. With that wealth of experience, my panic button was about ready to go off. I kept telling myself, "If you just keep out of the deep stuff—keep in the ruts that are fairly bare, keep your cool, don't gun it all of a sudden—it will all turn out all right. And so it did, but not right off. You see, the problem with keeping in ruts was that I kept watching the ridges of deep stuff so that I wouldn't get into them, and that silly cycle kept heading right for them. I would grit my teeth and hope that the orange stuff would keep the gravel out and no cars were coming around the corner while I maneuvered to get back into the rut. You see, I didn't want to go fast if I was going to fall, so I kept it around 10 mph. You cycle riders understand.

Dad was so patient. Anyone knows that it is harder to maneuver one of those things at slow speeds, but what in the world does a person do in such a predicament? I finally realized that I just would have to speed up, so I was soon going 15 mph.

I noticed a farmhouse off to the right, and when Dad went by it, he woke up three watchdogs, and they evidently couldn't believe what they were seeing, because they all took out after me to see what was going on. I didn't think I should stop and tell them. In fact, I was absolutely filled with terror. One was a Siberian husky; one was a big black-and-white mixture, and the other was a German shepherd.

Evidently they were well rested and in great running shape. I kept my cool and didn't open the thing wide open, because I reasoned within myself that if I was lying on the ground full of gravel, they would have a great time, so I had better keep going at a reasonable speed. I sped up to 20 mph. They finally got tired and gave up the chase. I seriously considered stopping at a safe distance and sitting by the road and crying for awhile, but I decided that it would just spoil our good time, and besides, if I stopped, maybe I couldn't get the bike started again. I just wasn't good at kick-starting it, and I didn't want to wear out the helpless female role all at once. We kept on going.

It wouldn't have been too bad, but the sun got warmer, and have you ever had a hot flash in one of those orange suits on a hot day? Of course you haven't, but I thought I would just melt from the heat! I didn't, and soon I cooled off a bit, and suddenly there was some pavement again! It is the nicest stuff!

We soon came upon Eagle Fern Park and took a little drive through it along the river, then on to George. Fortunately there wasn't much traffic, and I was beginning to feel more confidence. There was a little wide place at the side of the road, and Dad motioned for me to pull off alongside him. I was seized with panic, but sure enough it worked. He told me that on the road just ahead there is a Model A Ford that he wants to look at sometime. I offered to go down there with him, but he said no, he would do that another day.

As we started out there was a hill, and not having learned my lesson well enough, I eased out and all went silent again. Suddenly I was filled with grit and determination and got the thing into neutral, got the kick starter into position, and gave it the works! Soon it was purring again, and I was too. I was so glad that I followed Dad, because that way he missed seeing some of the extra maneuvers I performed. I didn't know for sure how much he could see in those rearview mirrors, but he didn't let on a bit.

Help, the pavement is gone again! Oh well, no problem, I have experience now! I even got up to 40 mph on the gravel. When I realized how fast I was going, I practically froze on the spot, but I soon got my brain to work again and told myself that everything was just fine—and it was.

I didn't know that a person could get saddle sore from riding a motorcycle; I really don't think that most people do, but I was so tense that I think the seat rubbed on the muscles that rubbed on the bones! I don't know what made me assume the bent back position that I did, unless I was trying to take advantage of the windshield, but I kept having the feeling when people passed us and waved, they could tell Dad was a man with some expertise, but that I was a woman with little experience. I kept thinking to myself, *Now, how can they tell, when I am covered head to toe the same as Dad!*

I began to realize that no man ever rode a motorcycle in that position, or in that manner. Well, next time I can work on handling it better. When we got home—oh, blissful moment—I apologized to him for holding him back, and he told me that it was a simply wonderful ride and he loved it. I knew that he meant it, and I loved it too. When we got home Dad went right down and bought me the best motorcycle battery available at the store!

"However, each one of you also must love his wife as he loves himself, and the wife must respect her husband" Ephesians 5:33 *NIV*.

Chapter 16

Forever Changed

1978

*O*ur lives were full to the brim with happiness. It was August 1, and Daryl and Diane had just returned from Indonesia, where they had spent a year as student missionaries. The twins were about to start high school, and our oldest, Duane, had started medical school that very day. Everett was busy, as usual, at the hospital. Life was beautiful. It was a balmy, sunshiny kind of time—until the phone rang.

As is our custom, we'd gathered in the living room after supper to read God's word and pray together. We call it family worship. The phone rang, and Diane slipped out to answer it. "Mother," she called out, "come quickly, something is wrong. It sounds like Daddy is crying!"

I knew instinctively that something had happened to Daryl. Since returning from Indonesia, he had done so much to brighten my life. He was the official "fix-it" man about the house and had spent that very day shaping things up. Then he'd left for a ride up to Mt. Hood that afternoon to test-drive a motorcycle on which he'd been working. He'd said, "Don't save supper, I'll eat later."

Earlier I'd seen an ambulance and then a sheriff's car go screaming past our home toward Mt. Hood. Later the ambulance had come racing back by, siren blaring, lights flashing, going very fast. Each time I said, "I wonder if Daryl has been hurt." Each time the other children chided me, "Oh, Mom, don't worry so much, he will be home soon."

Everett's voice on the phone jolted me back to the moment. His first words to me were, "Where is Daryl?" My heart was breaking as I said, "He's up at the mountain, checking out his motorcycle." Everett's reply was strained. "No he isn't; they're bringing him here in an ambulance." The emergency medical technicians with Daryl had called ahead to alert the neurosurgeon that they were bringing in a critical case. Everett had heard about the call, because he was working with the neurosurgeon that day.

It was a motorcycle accident; a Forest Service truck loaded with water had run over the victim's head. The patient's name was Daryl Wilson.

I paused with the children to plead for God's help. Then Diane and I headed for the hospital. The 25 miles seemed like a hundred. Thoughts flooded my heart, endless prayers ascended. Diane drove while I prayed. That day changed our lives forever.

We ran into the emergency department, looking for Daryl. He was in X-ray, so we stood in the hall outside the big doors and waited. Everett had been an anesthesiologist at this hospital for almost 30 years and we knew a lot of people who worked there. Everyone already seemed to know about our tragedy, and they offered us love and support. When the doors opened and they wheeled Daryl through, they stopped briefly when they saw us. He was in a deep coma and was decerebrate (his body and mind were not functioning together). His arms were rigid and pulled into his sides. They told me that he was on his way to surgery; that his left leg was badly cut and he was bleeding profusely. I kissed him and whispered in his ear that I loved him and was praying for him.

Diane and I followed him up to the surgery floor, and a nurse kindly invited us to wait just outside the big doors. We prayed and expressed our faith in God. Friends and staff stopped by to pray with us and comfort us. Everett went to surgery with Daryl. Three and a half hours later they brought Daryl through those big doors and took him to the recovery room. When they finally decided he was in good enough condition, they transferred him to the intensive care unit (ICU).

We followed him to ICU and spent time holding him and praying over him.

Everett joined us there. One of the other anesthesiologists took call the rest of the night, so Everett and I could be together with Daryl.

We learned that what had started out as a leisurely ride on a beautiful day by our 21-year-old son, in a split second had turned into what would be nine months of unconsciousness. The complications were many. The endless hours of waiting and trying to awaken Daryl took their toll on the entire family. The doctor cautioned me that it would be a long, long time before we would see any changes— maybe never. The fact that Daryl was young and strong and had led a clean life was in his favor. I spent hours at the hospital each day, while trying to hold the rest of the family together.

Everett continued his practice, but at every turn there were reminders of his son, lying just down the hall, totally unconscious. Daryl had been such a blessing; an athlete, a Christian, and a caring person. One of Daryl's friends sought out Everett later and asked if he was Daryl's dad. He said, "I just want to tell you that it is because of Daryl that I am a Christian today. Daryl showed me that you can be a Christian and have fun too." We appreciated his testimony.

The twins, Dave and Deb, had lost the brother they idolized. Mom and Dad were different too; not available, not able to participate in their young lives as much.

Diane was soon off to college, but she found it difficult to concentrate while trying to cope with her aching heart. Duane offered to give up medical school and come home to be with us, but we urged him to press toward his goal. There was really nothing he could do for Daryl. There was really nothing *any* of us could do but wait and pray.

Each of us dealt with our grief differently, unable to share our suffering with each other. We lacked the skills, and there was no time or energy to learn new behavior. We just struggled and survived.

Shortly after the accident I asked our pastor to anoint Daryl. He told me that he didn't think the timing was right. Several months later he called and said he knew of someone who he thought would anoint Daryl. I eagerly contacted that pastor, and we made all the appropriate arrangements for the service. It would be held in Daryl's room at the hospital. I had all the faith in the world that Daryl would be healed. I knew that the hospital help was watching. Daryl had been there, unconscious, for five months. His case was so sad and hopeless, I told myself, "what a wonderful opportunity for God to show His power by healing our son." I went to Daryl's closet and picked out his favorite clothes for him to wear home and carried them with me to the hospital. In my heart I knew that all things were possible with God.

We arrived early for the service, and I told the still unresponsive Daryl everything that was going to happen. His eyes were open, but they did not move or follow action, and his arms lay useless at his side. I was so excited! I knew that soon he would say, "Hi, Mom, I love you," and put his arms around me.

When the minister poured the oil on Daryl and prayed for him, I watched closely. The only response was that Daryl raised his right eyebrow a little—that was all! No eye movement, nothing. We quietly left the room. The nurses were watching us, and I controlled my tears momentarily, not wanting anyone to lose faith in God because of me. But once in the car the tears flowed freely. It felt good to cry. I prayed, "All right, Lord, who am I to tell you what to do and when to do it? You know the beginning from the end. Please give us the strength and the courage, and we will go on trusting in you. We still don't have the answers, but it is okay. We know that someday Daryl will run and jump again and be the same wonderful Christian that he was before, even if we have to wait for the New Earth."

Gradually we could detect signs that Daryl was gaining awareness. His eyes would open sometimes, but they did not yet follow movement. He couldn't swallow food of any kind, or talk. Each day when I went to the hospital to visit him, I would take him outside on a stretcher, weather permitting, and talk to him about the sky, the clouds, and the flowers.

They had just mowed the lawn one day and I reached down and picked up a handful of newly mowed grass and put it under his nose—hoping for a response. Nothing!

One day I parked his stretcher right in front of our diesel automobile, locked the stretcher in place, and started the engine, hoping the click-click sound of the diesel engine would evoke some response. I watched him closely; again he raised his right eyebrow ever so slightly. My fondest hope was that some of the sights, sounds, and smells would awaken his ability to communicate. We all talked to him as though he could hear us and gave him lots of hugs and reassurance, praying often with him.

We blew up balloons and tossed them around his room, hoping his eyes would follow them. We made posters and hung them around his room. We didn't think he looked at them, but much later he recited one of the poems from memory.

Nine months to the day after his accident I went to the dietician and asked her if she could think of anything I could try to feed Daryl—something she thought he might be able to swallow. All this time he had received all of his nourishment through a JJ tube, surgically inserted into his stomach. Through disuse, the muscles in his throat and neck no longer seemed to function at all. We had tried feeding him fruit juice, ice cream, applesauce, and Jello, to no avail. But she blended some celery soup until it was perfectly smooth, and I ran up to Daryl's room to share it with him. Slowly, with great effort, he was able to swallow about a half cup of it. What a great victory, the beginning of better things!

I had been bending over him for weeks asking, "Daryl, can you say 'Mom'?" For a couple of days I noticed his lips forming the word. Now, after he'd swallowed the soup, I said, "Daryl, please say 'Mom.'" My joy knew no bounds as I heard him say the word, "Mom!" The nurses shared in my excitement and enthusiasm as he repeated the word for them.

When the neurosurgeon stopped by that day, I told him about the soup. He said, "Daryl can't eat; I tried to feed him applesauce this morning and he couldn't swallow it."

But now the doctor ordered food for Daryl, and the diet kitchen sent up a lovely tray, artistically arranged with several different piles of colorful, pureed food. I exclaimed, "I think it is more than he can possibly eat all at once!"

The nurse assured me that the hospital could afford the expense; after all, Daryl hadn't eaten a bite for nine months.

This was the beginning of his return to reality. Nothing happened quickly, but two months later we were able to bring him home.

I threw myself wholeheartedly into the role of nurse, mother, caregiver, housekeeper, and wife. Daryl was paralyzed on his right side and had almost no sense of balance, and we could not understand his speech. Quickly my life turned into a 24 hour-a-day marathon. Days were tough, but nights were extremely hard for all of us.

One day I heard a gasping, gagging noise from the room where Daryl was sitting. A great amount of fuchsia-colored saliva was running down the front of him, and he couldn't seem to breathe. His skin color was definitely blue. I made a dash for the phone, called 911, grabbed a towel and handed it to him. He immediately tried to stuff his mouth full of it. I noticed a little, plastic container sitting next to him, and I remembered buying a little, bright-fuchsia colored stick of material at the fair, to rub over glass to keep it from fogging.

Daryl had a sweet tooth, and I assumed that he thought it was candy and had put it in his mouth. I didn't know what the stick was made of, but evidently it had a very burning effect. The emergency medical technicians arrived shortly. They gave Daryl CPR and got him breathing again, then looked me in the eye and gravely said that they would have to transport him to the hospital.

The case would be investigated as an attempted suicide. I cried out in disbelief, "No, it can't be; Daryl just thought it was candy!" They replied, "Sorry, Lady, we are required to take him in and do some tests."

I followed the ambulance to the hospital, where they did the required tests, which proved inconclusive. The EMTs and I were of separate opinions still, but the good thing was that Daryl was all right and probably wouldn't have any adverse effects from ingesting the material. Of course, I offered a sincere prayer of thanksgiving, and Daryl joined me in the prayer.

Even though I felt God's presence, I was shattered. I had failed terribly and now felt scared and helpless. I sat down to try to collect my wits, and thought, "Who can I call? I can't call my husband; he's in surgery. The other children are away at school. I don't have any friends. I've been so totally consumed in taking care of Daryl, that I had not developed any interests outside the home."

I could not leave unless I took him with me, and that limited my movement. At that moment I realized that there was nobody I could call. What a desolate feeling.

I didn't have the energy, the strength, or the time to get involved in anything else. But I felt impressed that if anything was going to change, I was going to have to do something about it myself. I gave it a lot of thought and prayer and felt impressed to call Becky, a woman who was leading a Bible study group for woman at our church. I'd stayed away from the meetings, because Daryl was a man and his major head injuries and mental deficits led him to sometimes make strange noises and say inappropriate things.

But when I asked Becky if it would be all right if I brought Daryl to the study group, she was thoughtful and even excited that I would ask. As I attended those studies at our church, I began to emerge little by little out of the hole I was in, and began to see that there were others out there who cared. I began to develop friends I could call when the need arose, and say, "I can hardly handle life today," and they would listen. I didn't go to the studies to cry on their shoulders all the time; I just listened as we studied the Word of God. It was a real blessing to me; the beginning of living again.

The whole family was hurting, not only because Daryl was in this situation, but because I, the wife and mother, was consumed with grief and preoccupied with trying to help Daryl get better.

About two years after the accident, I was taking Daryl to outpatient therapy in a van we had purchased to accommodate him and his wheelchair. It had a lift and tie-downs, but he didn't like to ride in his chair, because he could only talk very softly, and I couldn't hear him from the driver's seat. He'd begged to sit in the front on the passenger side, and I finally agreed. When we arrived at the hospital where he would have his therapy, I got his wheelchair out of the van and parked it beside the open passenger door. I was assisting him in the way I always did when somehow I twisted and injured my back. Pain shot through me like a knife. I couldn't move. A cheery female voice asked, "May I help you?" It was a physical therapist, and I had just breathed a prayer for help. She pushed Daryl to his therapy appointment, and as I began to feel relief, I followed.

Daryl was six feet tall and weighed 180 pounds. I wondered, "Now what, Lord? How can I take care of my son if I can't even transfer him in and out of his wheelchair?"

I quickly made an appointment with Daryl's neurosurgeon to have my back checked out. Tests showed that I had pushed two disks out between the vertebrae and needed to have surgery. I was anxious to get it done quickly so I could go on caring for Daryl. Diane flew over from Boise to take care of him while I was in the hospital, and she stayed for a few days afterward to help out. The surgery brought excellent results, and I didn't have any more back pains for 15 years.

As we adjusted to this new life, I began to notice changes in our adopted children, Dave and Deb, that I didn't understand—big changes involving anger, dishonesty, and lying. It hurt so much. I had no idea how to deal with the problem, because I didn't even know what the problem was. Finally, in desperation I told Dave that he would either have to leave home or accept counseling. He chose counseling.

I was shocked by what the counselor learned. Dave was an alcoholic and needed intensive treatment.

I knew nothing about alcoholics, except what I saw in Old Town— poor, downtrodden human beings, propped up against buildings, or on the sidewalks, clutching wine bottles. My son was not like these people! We had never had alcohol in our home; neither had either of our families.

As Dave's treatment progressed, I was required to go for counseling and group therapy, twice a week, 40 miles away. The voice on the other end of the line said, "You will learn all about alcoholism." I made it clear to the voice that I didn't want to learn about alcoholism, that I had never tasted alcohol, and that I had a severely injured son I could not leave alone. The voice said, "You have to do it—for your son!" So I did it!

The day we finished paying for Dave's treatment, the phone rang and a voice said, "Your daughter, Deb, is an alcoholic and needs to go for treatment—now." My knees buckled, as pain and anxiety overwhelmed me. Would anything ever be all right again? Would I ever feel that sunshiny, balmy feeling again?"

1984

Until the time of Daryl's accident, we had been good stewards and had put away money consistently to provide for our retirement. But shortly after the accident our stockbroker highly recommended that we see a financial counselor. He was kind and full of empathy. In our state of emotional need, his understanding and caring appealed to us, and we agreed to work with him, after he assured us that he would not spend our money, only advise us.

He said, "After all, you shouldn't have to worry about handling your finances when you are under so much stress."

After working with the advisor for a period of time, we began to feel uneasy about the overall investment picture. We tried to separate ourselves from the structure he had created, but alas, we had signed guarantees for some rather large building projects; there was no way to back out now.

Our trusted advisor turned out to be far less than the scrupulous man we had believed him to be. Later he was tried and convicted of income tax evasion and served prison time.

Meanwhile we were forced to go through bankruptcy, because the guarantees we had signed on the advice of this advisor were joint and several. Not in a lifetime could we have paid off the millions of dollars that were demanded of us.

The pain and humiliation sent Everett into a depression we could hardly endure. He had a hard time carrying on with his work; his mind just didn't seem to function as it once had.

Meanwhile, I was still full-time caregiver for Daryl, but because of the bankruptcy, I realized that I would have to contribute to our income. Selling real estate would not only help financially, it would also give me some outside contact, which I desperately needed. By this time I could leave Daryl alone for two or three hours at a time. He had relearned some speaking skills, so if he had a problem, he could call my beeper or cell phone from the portable phone he carried on his electric wheelchair.

I called him frequently to be sure he was all right. If he didn't answer, I'd hurry home to check things out. One day there was no answer, so I told the customer who was in the car with me that I would need to go by my house and check on my son. The house was quiet and there was no answer to my calls. I began to search the yard and saw his wheelchair lying on its side at the top of a bank. I ran to the car and asked my customer to come help me. Daryl had fallen out of his chair and rolled down the bank. The phone was still in the wheelchair. Between us we were able to get him back into the house. It was a stressful way to live.

Our family was clearly dysfunctional; Daryl couldn't walk or care for himself, my grief was overwhelming—I did not know how to deal with life from day to day. Our marriage relationship was distant, and inside, our souls were barren.

God was always my refuge in the time of storm, but I was overwhelmed. There were so many things I didn't know about prayer, yet I knew there was a God who loved me, and I talked to Him a lot. I gave lip service to my faith, and I knew that, somehow,

His way was best. There seemed no way out of this heartbreaking situation.

Then I learned to pray—to really pray. The windows of heaven opened, and the sunshine came back. I went to a Christian Women's Retreat. There I learned about a prayer where I surrendered all to God, gave Him my anger and pain, and asked Him to fill the void with His gifts. I began to dedicate a special time each day to prayer and Bible study; to focus my prayer life, to be specific. I began to journalize my prayers each day, using my computer. I began to know the joy again of answered prayer in little things.

It surprised me to see the difference in my family after I learned to pray and let God take control of my life. Everett began communicating to me in all sorts of little ways that he loved me and appreciated me, and the children each began communicating more with us and with each other.

I began to put more effort into mothering and grandmothering. I picked out a special box for each grandchild—something I thought he or she would like. Some were plastic lunchboxes with fun things painted on them; others were boxes covered with brightly colored paper. I wrote each child's name on a box with a permanent marker.

From time to time I would come across something I thought one of the children would like and I would slip it into the appropriate box. One time I put a signed picture of me in each box. Another time it was a note from me telling him or her how blessed I was to be their grandma. When I knew they were coming, I would make sure I had a special treat for them in their boxes. Each time any of the grandchildren came to our house, they would make a mad dash to the mystery box cupboard. The little ones have grown up now, but they have fond memories of the mystery boxes.

1991

After 13 years as caregiver, our children urged us to make other living arrangements for Daryl. They told me that the rest of the family needed more of me, and they felt that it was too hard for me to give him fulltime care; besides, he needed to be around other young people. It was hard for me to even think about it. I knew in my heart that nobody else would give him the kind of care I was giving him, but we agreed to look at options. Persons with head injuries are prone to outbursts, and this makes it hard to find caregivers for them.

Diane found a facility in Boise where she lived that had an opening in their Head Injury Unit. We interviewed them and asked Daryl what he thought about it. He was eager and wanted to get on with life. We took him to his new location in December and left him there. After we dried our tears, we found it fun and exciting to just talk to one another without interruption. We were free to do things together; to go for a walk, to shop for groceries, to go bicycling. We put the house up for sale so we could move the 400 miles to Boise to be near Daryl and give him hugs and outings.

We visited Daryl in February and found him all hunched over in his wheelchair, drooling. He'd lost 25 pounds. Oh, how my heart ached! I wanted to take him right back home with us. We talked together and prayed about it and spoke with the nurses and the doctor. They had put him on heavy doses of Haldol to control his outbursts, but they promised to cut back on his medication.

We intermittently cried all the way back to Portland and plunged full speed into getting our home sold and making the move. We knew that our Lord would make what seemed impossible, possible in His time.

"Verily, verily, I say unto you, that ye shall weep and lament, but the world shall rejoice; and ye shall be sorrowful, but your sorrow shall be turned into joy" John 16:20 *KJV*.

Daryl, circa 1980

My Forever Friend

No Treatment – No Cure

Book 3

Chapter 17

The Prayer of Faith

*I*n a few months we sold the house, Everett announced his retirement, and we moved to Boise. Finding no house with wheelchair access that would accommodate our needs, we decided to have a house built. What fun to plan it, build it, and then move in! Neither of us had ever lived in a brand new house before.

We landscaped it ourselves, in the manner of Ma Holt's old-fashioned garden that I loved as a child. Everett had made arrangements to get his medical license activated in Idaho, and I was able to get my Real Estate Broker's license by reciprocity.

Everett worked two days a week in a day surgery setting, which meant no night calls and no weekend calls. It seemed like an endless vacation. He played a lot of golf. I started my own real estate company and did well.

We celebrated our 50th wedding anniversary in 1997, recounting the Lord's blessings to us with our family and friends. Duane and Linda and their family came all the way from Longview, Washington. They brought some puppets and put on a great show for us—what fun!

1997

For three years in a row I had had pneumonia at least once, and a few days after my latest visit to the doctor, his nurse called and asked me to come in for more X-rays. I told her that I had just had quite a few X-rays, but she said the doctor wanted to check for something else. So I went in for the X-rays, and a couple of days later the doctor informed me in his office that something was wrong with my lungs, and referred me to a pulmonologist.

On my visit to the lung specialist, I learned that I probably had a disease that could only be diagnosed for sure by surgical biopsy—a lung condition known as Idiopathic Pulmonary Fibrosis, or IPF. He said that the X-rays showed typical "velcro tare rales" on the lower right side of my chest.

I had never heard of such a condition, and I plied him with questions. He explained that the only cure was a lung transplant, and that I was now past the age to receive such a transplant. He suggested that I talk things over with my husband and decide if I wanted to have the biopsy done. He explained that if indeed I did have IPF, statistically I did not have long to live.

Duane and Linda visited us, and we told them about our dilemma. Duane had accepted the role of caregiver for Daryl, when the time came that we were unable to care for him. We told them about my prognosis and expressed our concern that perhaps he would have to assume that role soon. I reminded them that Daryl needed to be in a place where he would have a support system and lots of hugs and laughs.

Duane immediately asked if we would be willing to move to Longview. We thought about it for a few minutes and told them that, yes, if they could find a place for Daryl where he would enjoy as good or better care than he was receiving in Boise.

As we prayed about it, we reminded the Lord that Daryl was becoming more and more reticent to go back to his quarters after visiting our home, saying, "Are you going to make me go back to that prison?"

After only a few days, Duane called and asked if I could fly over the next day to interview the owners of a prospective home for Daryl. I told him I would be there. We were impressed with the facility and made arrangements to move Daryl there the following week. We quickly put our lovely new home on the market and began searching for a place to live in the Longview area. We wanted to be supportive of Daryl as long as we could.

2000

After we moved and got settled, I began feeling more and more short of breath. Our driveway was about 400 feet long and a little hilly. I soon found that I couldn't walk all the way to and from the house to the mailbox, without sitting down to rest for a while. When I'd lean over to make the bed, I also found it difficult to breathe. Often when someone called on the phone they would say, "Why are you so out of breath?"

Then I remembered that the doctor in Boise had told me to see a pulmonologist right after we got moved, so I made an appointment and poured out my story to my new doctor. He asked if I would be willing to have a biopsy, and I assured him that I would. It comforted me to know that Duane was on the staff at St. John's Hospital, where the surgery would be done. After the surgery, when I went back to see my doctor, he briskly walked into the room and said, "Our diagnosis of IPF has been confirmed by surgical biopsy. There is no treatment and no cure."

Everett was with me when the doctor uttered this sentence, and the two of us just sat there and looked at each other, as the doctor explained that my life expectancy was two to four years. He said he would do all he could to help me, and put me on Prednisone. I didn't like the way it made me feel and look, so he eventually changed the medication to Azathiaprine. It didn't seem to have the side effects that bothered me.

I jumped right into a pool of denial. But after having it all explained to me again, and reading up on it, I began to realize that this was serious business. I signed up for water aerobics at the YMCA, and asked the doctor if I should go two or three times a week. He said, "No, four or five times."

A friend told me about a machine that emitted radio frequency rays and suggested that I try it. I could not find any record of it having been used for this disease, but I was anxious to give it a try. IPF is considered a rare disease, with only about 83,000 diagnosed cases in the United States as of 2005. This meant that very little research had been done done, so I used the machine faithfully, though it was hard to tell what, if anything, it was doing for my lungs.

What I did know is that most of my life I had been a vegetarian and that I loved fruits and vegetables. I'd always paid attention to my diet, I'd never smoked or drank, and I made it a point to get lots of sleep, and drank lots of water.

Shortly after the biopsy, I contacted our pastor and asked if he would anoint me, claiming the promise of James 5:14,15 *NIV* that "the prayer of faith shall save the sick." He agreed and suggested that we do it at a meeting he was having at the church the following week.

We prepared our hearts, and at the meeting Pastor Dave asked me to come forward and sit on a chair. He then invited the local elders to come forward and surround me. As he placed the oil on my forehead, he earnestly asked the Lord to forgive my sins and to work out His will in my life and to heal me if He saw fit. It gave me peace that our son Duane was one of the elders who took part in the service.

That night I woke up at 2 a.m. and discovered that I could breathe easier and wasn't wheezing. I shook Everett awake and asked him to get his stethoscope and listen to my chest to see how my lungs sounded. They sounded great, he said, except for the "Velcro tare rales" that were still audible in the lower right lung. I couldn't wait to tell my doctor.

When I saw him again, I asked him if he was a Christian and he said, "Yes." I mentioned James 5 and told him I had been anointed. He smiled and shook his head: "Nobody gets cured from IPF."

We'd now bought a nice little home with several huge, heated shops, on two acres. One acre was covered with tall fir trees. The other acre had a lot of room for a nice garden. Everett was thrilled with the shops and the garden potential. He built a small greenhouse and raised loads of good strawberries, raspberries, thornless blackberries, grapes, apples, plums, and vegetables. I loved planting a lot of beautiful flowers, including roses, lupines, lilies, and cosmos. It made me think of Mother, and I enjoyed the peace I had found.

I began to realize that I was getting weaker, and I thought how nice it would be to live in town, close to the YMCA and to neighbors and church members who might drop by to see me. Everett and I talked about it, and it was clear that Everett did not want to leave our home in the country where he could work on cars and equipment, to his heart's content. On the other hand, what I said made some sense. We were spending a lot of time, money, and energy driving back and forth. I called our Realtors, and they began showing me different houses, but none of them filled the bill.

Any house we chose would need at least two bedrooms, wheelchair access, and either have a shop or room for one. It would also need to have its utility room on the main floor. Ed, a friend from church, called me one day and said, "You should look at the house across the street from us. It even has a six-foot-wide wheelchair ramp up to the front door." I wondered what it looked like, so I asked our Realtors to show it to me.

2001

When I stepped in the front door and looked out over the city through the large windows in the living room, I noticed that it had a warm, cozy feeling. I liked it.

When Everett and I went back to look at it together, I asked two good friends from church who had interior designing skills to join us.

All four of us liked what we saw. The house featured lots of honey colored woodwork, and the whole house just felt good. To Everett's disappointment, it had no shop, but he agreed that he could put two large sheds on the property and make do.

We began negotiating with the owner. The house was full of furniture and the cupboards were full, though the 85-year-old owner was now living in California. We made an offer for the house and everything in it, just as it was, and she accepted.

We now tackled the job of downsizing and selling all the extra stuff we now owned. It seemed wise to sell all that we could at our home in the country, because there was no room whatsoever for any more furniture in our new home. I knew that even though I was knowledgeable about sales and antiques—I had owned and operated two antique stores—I no longer had the energy and strength to manage this sale. I talked it over with Everett, and he said he would help some, but that he had made commitments with a group of men from our church and didn't want to give that up.

As I sorted through what to take and what to keep, I decided that I should open up our ping-pong table and lay out the things I wanted to sell. I rolled the folded table over to the middle of the shop floor and tried to open it, but it seemed stuck. So I give it a little yank to see if the lock would release. The next thing I knew, I was lying flat on the concrete floor, with the ping-pong table on top of me. Excruciating pain shot through my back and left leg. My mind was racing as I realized that Everett was going to be leaving for the church any minute now, and he didn't even know I was hurt. The doors were closed, and though I screamed, nobody heard.

Then I remembered that I still had a portable phone from the house in my pocket. Since I didn't know how to call my own home number, I called 911. The dispatcher was kind and asked if I wanted her to send an ambulance. I explained that no, my husband was a doctor, and if she would just call our house and tell him I was hurt out in the shop, he would know what to do.

When he opened the shop door, he said that my face was as white as a sheet. He immediately turned up the heat, lifted the table off of me, and began to check me over for broken bones. He decided that it would be safe to transport me himself, so he ran to the house and brought back a wheelchair. My back hurt a lot, but there was no paralysis in my arms or legs. He carefully lifted me into the wheelchair and gently pushed me to the house. Since there were no steps, he was able to wheel me right into the bedroom and place me on the bed.

He was supposed to be at the church, practicing for a *Journey to the*

Cross program in which he would be playing the part of Nicodemus, and I insisted that I would be fine and that he should go ahead. But not long after he left, the pain got worse, so I decided to get into the Jacuzzi tub in our bedroom, turn it on, and see if that helped. But I soon realized that the pain was only getting worse. So with great effort I made it back to the bed and the phone. I called the church and asked the person who answered to find my husband, while I held the line. When Everett answered, I asked, "Do you want me to call an ambulance, or do you want to come home and take me to the hospital?" He said he would come and take me. The pain was becoming intolerable.

We had a Lexus coupe, and Everett arranged the back seat so I could almost lie down as we traveled. He drove gently all the way, though I'd groan at every little bump. When we got to the hospital and the nurse rolled me briskly over a bump at the threshold, I let out a yell. I didn't mean to, I just couldn't help it. Once inside they took me directly to an examining table. When the doctor came in, he took one look at my face and ordered morphine for me. Everett had already filled him in about the details of my condition.

The morphine helped control the pain as they took me to X-ray. Sure enough, they found several compression fractures in my spine. My left leg had a long abrasion, where the edge of the table had scraped down my leg, but it wasn't broken. Was I glad! Then they discharged me and told me to take it easy. For several days the pain was so severe that the pain medication itself kept me quiet. But as the pain eased, I had to work hard to take it easy. It just didn't come naturally.

"Therefore my heart is glad, and my glory rejoiceth; my flesh also shall rest in hope" Psalm 16:9 *KJV*.

Chapter 18

Roots

2002

My mind kept going back to that unsolved piece of my life puzzle—I wanted to find out more about my roots on my biological father's side. It seemed that half of me was missing. I rarely spoke of it, but in my heart I really wanted to find out who he was.

I did some research to determine if I had the name right—George Unselt. I'd made sure not to forget it, since I'd first heard it at age 16. But I'd rarely ever uttered the name out loud. When I'd asked my mother about him, she'd emphatically said she'd never heard of him. The two aunts who had given information about him to my roommate were no longer living. So I contacted some of their descendants who might have heard stories, but evidently the topic had been taboo. I called Aunt Cleda, Daddy's sister. She confirmed the name and where this man had lived, but she could provide little other information.

Recently I came across Daddy's death certificate and noticed that the secondary cause of death was pulmonary fibrosis. My heart skipped a beat. IPF has sometimes been shown to run in families. Maybe Daddy really was my father. How could I find out? I began making phone calls and looking on the Internet for information about DNA matching. I found out that if I could get DNA samples from my brother, sister, and mother, they could be compared with my own DNA and I could know for sure if Daddy was my biological father. The cost to me would be $900.

Al and Cathie agreed to participate, and I swabbed Mother's mouth when I went to see her. After all the specimens were sent in, I eagerly awaited the results. When the estimated date of arrival for these results passed, I began meeting the mailman every day—but after a couple of weeks of this, still no letter had arrived.

So I called the company and learned that they had just compiled the results and could fax them to me. I gave them my fax number and stood over the machine in eager anticipation. If Daddy was really my father, I had spent all these years in needless pain.

The phone rang, and I bent over the fax machine, reading each word as it came out: "Al and Cathie were children of the same man, but Roen had a different father."

My knees buckled and I sank into my chair. I couldn't cry. I was alone. No, not alone. My Best Friend heard all about it as I poured out my heart in prayer. Of course He already knew, but He gave me peace and comfort.

When Everett came home, I told him what I had learned, and he assured me that it didn't matter—that he loved me just the same and didn't care who my father was. Those were nice words to hear, but it mattered to me—a lot.

2004

Diane called one day and said that she had found George Unselt's name on a genealogy site on the Internet. I was stunned and excited. I quickly checked it out and found that the wife of one of George Unselt's nephews was doing research on the German roots of the large Unselt family. Thanks to the computer, I was able to get her phone number, and I gave her a call.

She was most helpful. I had already obtained a copy of George Unselt's birth and death certificates. She added quite a lot to the picture. I asked her if George Unselt had ever been a Christian.

She replied, "I don't know, but did you know that he was a member of the Mob?"

"What's the Mob?" I asked.

"You know, the Mob," she replied. She said she would send me some pictures and newspaper articles. Within a week I received several pictures of George Unselt. I could see some family resemblance, but she had been unable to send any newspaper articles.

Diane and her husband, Jim, agreed to go with us to the San

Francisco Bay area to do some more research. Everett reluctantly agreed to go along, reminding me again that it didn't matter to him who my father was. Jim had grown up in the Bay area, so he chauffeured us around like a pro. We went to libraries, newspaper offices, the mortuary where George Unselt's body had been taken, a cemetery, the county courthouse, the assessor's office, the historical society, and the National Archives and Records Administration (NARA). We made copious notes and took pictures of the house George Unselt had lived in for 37 years, as well as businesses he had run.

It all proved exhausting for me, but I felt an inner drive to discover as much as I could. It all seemed overwhelming now. I organized a large notebook with the certificates, census records, pictures, newspaper clippings, homestead certifications, many letters, and a copy of the guest list from George Unselt's funeral (there had been a total of seven registered attendees).

I tried to form a mental picture of this man. Who was he? Was he kind, happy, jealous, angry? Did he ever know Jesus?

One of my relatives told me that my mother had tried to talk George Unselt into leaving his wife of less than a year to marry her. He'd supposedly refused to do that. But as far as I can find out, I am his only offspring. I thanked the Lord for the information He had helped me find and promised Him that whatever time I had left, I would do my best to bring others joy and show them His love. I found peace.

I read and reread Jeremiah 1:5 *NIV*: "Before I formed you in the womb I knew you, before you were born I set you apart."

God knew me before I was born and had a plan for me. *What were you thinking, Lord? Maybe someday I'll know.*

Chapter 19

Going Into Business

A young man at our church helped with Daryl while we were in the process of getting settled in Longview. His name was Garland.

I asked him if he would be willing to help me hold a sale at our new house. He said he would love to and that he had considerable experience with such things. As it turned out, he was joy to work with and most helpful. David and several of his friends also came and helped. We were able to sell most of what the former owner had left in the house, plus some of our own things we didn't need anymore.

One customer from Vancouver identified himself as a dealer. He picked out several choice pieces of furniture and some nice smaller items and asked if I would accept a check in payment. I told him I would. It was Martin Luther King Day, so the banks were closed and I couldn't call and verify whether he had an account, and if it had funds. But we trusted him and allowed him to load the things into his pickup and drive away. The next morning, first thing, I took my checks to the bank and asked the teller to verify that the check for $1,200 from the young dealer was good. It turned out that there was no such account—the check was worthless. What a disappointment!

After the sale we donated the leftovers to charity, then began the huge job of cleaning the new house and arranging our things in it. Once again, Garland was a tremendous help. He also cleaned our country home for us.

Sometimes when I would ask one of my doctors if he felt I was strong enough to take a long journey or do some other energy taxing activity, he'd reply, "What have you got to lose?" It bothered me. I knew my prognosis was not good, but I wanted to take the best care of myself that I could, and I knew God would work out His will in my life as He saw fit.

I continued my routine at the YMCA and made some wonderful Christian friends there. Long ago in my daily conversations with the Lord, I had made it a point each day to ask Him to help me be a blessing to someone. Sometimes I'd recognize who that someone was; at other times I didn't—and that suited me just fine. On many occasions I had the opportunity to talk with people about the pain in their lives or invite them to outreach programs at our church. One day there were five of us from the YMCA all sitting together in our church, having a blessed time together. Now, when I go back after missing a few days at the YMCA, someone will say, "We missed your smile." Recently I have changed my prayer: I now say, "Help me to be a blessing to others today."

Our friends Helen and Marv came to spend a few happy days with us. My back began to hurt a lot—so bad I had to take medication to control the pain. Even then, I could hardly stand it. Helen pitched right in and did the cooking and cleaned the kitchen, and Marv helped Everett with a project. Then Helen took me to the doctor's office and to the drugstore to have a prescription filled. I became a regular customer at Duane's radiology office; fortunately, the X-rays showed no new breaks, just muscle spasms.

Daryl was doing fine in his new home and seemed content. The owners told us that they wanted to find a second house to rent and start another care facility. We told them we would buy a house for them to rent, if they could find the right place. So we sold some rental property in Boise and rolled it over into some rental property in Longview.

The caregivers found a house that we all thought would be suitable, so we bought the home and rented it to them. Daryl was moved to the new home.

2004

About six years after our move, the caregiver phoned us one day and asked us to meet him at his office. When we arrived, he got right to the point. He was going to make a change and wanted his manager to live on-site, with her family, at the home where Daryl was staying. This meant that three clients would have to leave, and Daryl was to be one of those who would need to go. We asked the business owner where Daryl would be moved, and he told us that would be our problem.

We knew that Daryl was considered "heavy care," but we hadn't expected that he would be turned away like this. So we quickly told the business owner that we would call him later, and made a hasty exit.

Linda, Duane's wife, drove me to interview several care facility operators, to try to find a new place for Daryl. But the results were discouraging. Someone mentioned a good place across state, but we were not in a position to be uprooted again.

Then Diane suggested that we license the home ourselves, hire a manager, and give notice to the former care operators to move. It seemed like a daunting order to fill. I was having extreme back and leg pain. So we continued to fill out forms and explore other possibilities. But as we prayed about it and asked for help and guidance, everything seemed to be telling us to run the home ourselves.

While Garland was helping me with the sale, he'd mentioned that he'd cleaned homes professionally for several people. I asked him if he would have time every other week to come in for a few hours and clean our home. He said he had the time and would like to help us.

Garland happened to be cleaning our house the very day we decided to go ahead and run the home where Daryl was living. So I asked Garland if he would be interested in being our manager. He said, "No, my health is not good enough, but maybe my wife would like the job." Lorie, his wife, was working in a large care facility as recreation director, and was ready to move on.

Lorie called me the next morning and told me she had hardly slept that night, thinking of the possibility of managing our care home.

Garland and she had previously owned such a house, and she had all the necessary credentials. We were acquainted with her work ethic and the way she handled responsibility. After a few family conferences, we hired Lorie. What a blessing she has been.

We gave the former managers notice to move out by September 1. All of the clients were developmentally disabled, except Daryl, who was also the only one confined to a wheelchair. While the manager was away, we looked the place over and were dismayed to find it in bad condition, with holes in the floor, walls, and ceiling.

They had put tile on the floor and walls in the shower room, but had not put a pan to catch any water that would seep through the tile onto the wood beneath. We found water damage in three adjoining rooms and ended up replacing the floor joist under the shower room, as well as many other boards. The roof was leaking in the family room. Now the bills were mounting. I was arranging for the different contractors to come in and do the work, when the pain in my back became unbearable. So I took time out to visit a neurosurgeon, and he recommended surgery.

We talked it over with the family, and David stepped up to the plate and volunteered to take care of Daryl while I was recovering, and to act as contractor, dealing with the various workers who were repairing the house. Dave did a great job, and the house repairs moved forward.

My IPF created a problem for those who would perform my surgery. My lung capacity was markedly decreased, and the doctors knew that other IPF patients at times were unable to wean themselves off a ventilator, after surgery.

One of my doctors said flatly, "No, don't do it," but offered no alternative for the pain except powerful drugs. My other doctor said, "Go ahead, but be sure to explain to the anesthesiologist ahead of time about the IPF."

We scheduled the surgery, asking our Heavenly Father to give direction to the anesthesiologist, as well as the surgeon. We asked Him to watch over me, and that His will be done. The anesthesiologist recommended a treatment with Albuterol just prior to surgery, and when all was said and done, I came through the surgery just fine and was able to breathe without the respirator shortly after arriving in the recovery room. There was much rejoicing in our family. My neurosurgeon had done bone grafts on my spine twice before, but these had not given me the relief I needed. This time he put in a metal plate and four long screws. The pain disappeared. God had made the impossible, possible!

The muscles spasms in my back still came and went. Everett massaged them often and provided some relief, but my back doctor said that a new procedure called vertebroplasty was now helping relieve back spasms. A traditional incision would not be necessary, but three holes would be made, through which instruments could be introduced to straighten up the more serious of the compression fractures I had sustained a few years earlier. A cement-type material would then be introduced to hold things together, as it hardened. We did some research and then decided to go for it. It required an anesthetic, but again, our prayers were answered, and I got along fine.

As I recovered, I was able to answer questions and make business decisions as needed. By January we had our license and had passed inspections by both the city and state. The house looked lovely, with its new coat of paint inside and out, new coverings on all the floors, and attractive furniture that we had picked up at garage sales.

We were licensed for six clients, including Daryl, and we were soon up to capacity, and stayed that way. Social Security now provided financial assistance for most of Daryl's care, and this was a great help, since our insurance had run out and Everett was now retired. The Boise care home had offered to contact the state on our behalf and ask regarding the availability of a supplement to pay the balance for Daryl's care. We didn't like to think that we couldn't take care of him ourselves, but clearly our strength and resources were no longer up to the task.

Lorie hired our son David and two other young people to work in our facility. Daryl enjoys having the young people around, especially his brother Dave. They frequently laugh and joke together, and take time to pray on a regular basis. Not once after visiting our home has Daryl ever asked not to be taken back to his own house.

"Weeping may endure for a night, but joy cometh in the morning" Psalm 30:5 *KJV*.

Chapter 20

My Legacy

2005

*D*iane and I were chatting one cold February day, and I mentioned that after my funeral I wanted her to invite close friends and family over for a party and give them the memory books that I was preparing for them. She thought it over for a few moments, then said, "I have a better idea. Why not have the party before you die so you can enjoy it too." *That would be unusual; I wonder if we could pull it off.*

My file drawers were full of trivia, photos, school accomplishments, and other items especially significant to me. I decided to create a three-inch binder for each of my loved ones and dearest friends, filled with as many memories as possible. Colorful, acid-free paper served as a background for the pictures and cards, which I then slipped into sheet protectors. Our son-in-law Jim then made a computer-generated name to put on the outer spine of each book. I included a personal letter with each book, telling the recipients how special they were to me and to God. I challenged them to give of their best to God and to others and assured them of my love and prayers.

The idea of having a party appealed to me. We could have it around Christmas time and give out the books in lieu of presents. As December drew near, I put more and more time and planning into the party. Daryl's birthday would be Saturday night, December 17. Why not have the party then? He would love the attention. He agreed that he really didn't need anything new, and that he would like to help others in lieu of gifts. So we agreed to put a note on the invitations, asking that those who wished to honor Daryl's 49th birthday bring a card, and slip in a contribution toward a much-needed new refrigerator for our school. Daryl loved the idea and so did the school.

Who should we invite? Family, friends, the whole church? Would I have the strength and energy to put it all together? We decided at last to invite only family and friends who had made a sizeable impact on our lives. We reserved the fellowship hall at the church, and I asked my friends Joe and Judy to take charge of preparing a light meal for the evening. They gladly accepted.

As we planned together, I asked Joe if he would help me shop for a refrigerator and told him of our plan. Joe was enthusiastic and said, "Roen, you don't have to go with me, we will find one." What a relief! Shopping for anything from a wheelchair can be complicated.

Joe did a lot of research, and he and Judy stopped by the school in person to determine the exact size of household-style refrigerator the school would need. While they were there, however, a Public Health Department inspector came by the school and mentioned that the Health Department required a commercial model for the school's institutional kitchen. What a shock! Would we be able to raise three times the amount of money we had at first envisioned? We moved forward in faith, however, and Joe was able to find just the right commercial model, at the best available price, and have it delivered to the school by the Wednesday before the party. After the gifts were tallied, we rejoiced that the refrigerator was not only installed and functioning already at the school, but was now paid for in full.

At the party we enjoyed a delicious light meal of soup, artisan bread, veggies, and pumpkin bars, all made by friends and family. We had covered the tables with white wrapping paper and used the sheets to write on as we played Hangman and other games. Holly cut from our tree adorned the tables. Each table also had a canning jar filled with brightly colored paper cones, bearing words of wisdom for those who happened to draw them. It was an evening of fun, music, and games.

When Daryl arrived, we tied a Happy 49th Birthday balloon to his wheelchair, and he smiled—his typical, lovely smile. David served as emcee, and I asked that he and Deb sing *He'll Rise Again*. Whenever they sing that song to Deb's accompaniment, I get goose bumps. Deb was not feeling well that evening, and it meant a lot to me that she put forth the extra effort to come, sing, and play.

The crew then put two long tables on stage, covered them with white tablecloths, and displayed the 28 memory books, backside to the audience. Then, near the close of the party, I sat on a stool in front, as the crew passed me one book at a time to present to my dear friends and family members. Each came forward to receive his or her custom-made book—my legacy. I loved the hugs.

How is it with you? Can you rejoice in the comfort and love of my Friend Jesus? Talk to Him today; give Him your heart, He loves you. I am praying for you, dear reader. He makes the impossible, possible.

On page 276 of the book *The 360-Degree Leader*, by John Maxwell, appears this quote by St. Francis of Assisi: "Start doing what is necessary; then do what is possible; and suddenly you are doing the impossible.

"With man this is impossible but with God all things are possible" Matthew 19:26 *NIV*.

Chapter 21

Our Adventure

2006

*E*xcitement ran high that Friday morning in our household of seventy-somethings. Our son Duane and his wife, Linda, had invited us to spend the weekend with them at Sun River, in the high flatlands of Central Oregon. Everett and I love Sun River, and best of all, we were to have Duane and Linda all to ourselves for the weekend. What fun! They picked us up promptly at 11:15 a.m., and we had a joyous time catching up on family, community, and church news, as we traveled.

We arrived at about 6 p.m. After Linda served us a lovely supper, we sat around the fire for a while. But I began to feel very tired and weak and told them I needed to go to bed; it had been a long day for a largely stay-at-home lady.

Duane and Everett helped me up the stairs—slowly. By the time we reached the top, however, I felt so weak and my breathing had become so labored that my knees buckled. I looked down at my hands, and the nail beds looked blue. Everett asked me how I felt, and I told him I was very weak and that my left chest ached and that I felt a fluttering sensation there.

Duane came quickly to my side with a pulse oximeter (a device that measures oxygen level in the blood). He slipped it on my finger, and he and Everett couldn't believe what it said, so one of them slipped it on one of their own fingers. Yes, it was working okay. It showed my oxygen saturation to be only about 75 percent of what it should be. Duane rushed out to the car and returned with an oxygen tank that he carries with him in his airplane whenever he flies.

By now I was lying on the bed, and they hooked me up to the tank with a cannula that fit under my nose. My oxygen level began to rise—from the mid-70s into the mid-80s. I began to settle down, but I was very sleepy. Since the tank was equipped with safeguards for pilots, it had a built-in alarm that would sound if the person using it didn't breathe and activate the flow of oxygen. Every time I dozed off, the alarm on the tank would sound, and immediately Everett would say, "*Breathe*, you have got to *breathe!*"

I would try and try, but the alarm would still keep going off, telling us I wasn't breathing deeply enough to activate the oxygen.

I finally told Everett that it was too hard to breathe deeply enough—I was just too tired. He got an intense look on his face and gently said," It is either that, or tell me good-bye." So I assured him that I would work as hard as I could to breathe and that I wasn't going away.

It was hard to think clearly, but I knew I was in the best hands possible in that room and that I wanted God's will to be done. I didn't feel one moment of fear.

Everett called Duane back into the room, and they decided to put the mask on my face, hoping that way to deliver more oxygen to me. I am not fond of masks—in fact, I am inclined to panic. But I kept telling myself, "I can do this; I *will* do this if it is what it takes to carry on."

They found that even when I used the mask, the alarm would go off, but that if they held their fingers over the vents in the mask and held the mask more snugly against my face, all was well. Duane ran out to the car and got some black tape he had brought along, and they used it to cover the vents in the mask and to mold it more closely to my face. *Hooray, it worked!*

But now what? My two wonderful doctors agreed that the higher elevation (4,500 ft.) was causing my pronounced oxygen deficit. So, what were the options? We only had this one, small oxygen tank and didn't know how long the oxygen supply would last. They could take me to the hospital, but after I got stabilized, then what? It was a long way from where we were to a lower altitude. They could take turns doing CPR, but that was not practical to do in a car.

All things considered, it seemed best to move me quickly to a lower elevation, before the oxygen ran out. So Duane told Linda of the change in plans, and Everett brought up the wheelchair and helped me put on a coat. Linda stuck her head into my room, and I said, through the mask, "Oh, Honey, I am so sorry!"

She held her hand up to stop me from talking and said, "Not a word of it! We are having an adventure!" What a girl! At 1 a.m. we started for home.

Duane had consulted his GPS and discovered that the quickest way to get to a lower altitude was to drive north toward The Dalles, Ore. It was an excellent choice, because by taking that route, we also avoided a lot of ice and snow on other roads that early winter morning.

But everyone was now tired, and the three of them took short, frequent turns driving. We stopped at one point to get gasoline, and they wheeled me to the restroom. The poor filling station attendant working that dark, early morning, must have wondered if I was a ghost or an angel. I had on a long, white satin nightgown, a short black coat, and a clear oxygen mask with black electricians' tape patches.

We arrived home safe, sound, and exhausted at 6 o'clock that Saturday morning. By then my oxygen saturation was up to 90 percent. *Praise the Lord!* David advised me to go to the coast next time we wanted to get away. We live at about 50 ft. above sea level.

I asked Duane how he happened to have the tank and oximeter along with him, and he said, "I stuck them in, just in case".

God has many ways to take care of us. The doctor who diagnosed my lung condition so many years before had believed I had at most two to four years to live. But that was 10 years ago. This "thorn" has not been removed from my flesh, but God has dramatically slowed its progress. His grace is sufficient for me.

Rejoice, He makes the impossible, possible. And don't forget to smile, for life is always an opportunity, if God is on your side.

"Rejoice in the Lord always; and again I say, Rejoice" Philippians 4:4 *KJV*.

Smile!
Mark 10:27

My Dear Child:

Before I formed you in the womb I knew you and consecrated you.
Jeremiah 1:5
The very hairs of your head are all numbered. *Matthew 10:30*
I created you in My image. *Genesis 1:27*

I gave you life and breath and all things. *Acts 17:25*
You are My offspring. *Acts 17:28*
I wove you in your mother's womb. *Psalm 139:13*

I call you My Child, because I love you. *1 John 3:1*
I will, give what is good to those who ask Me. *Matthew 7:11*
Do not be anxious for tomorrow. *Matthew 6:34*

I have drawn you with lovingkindness. *Jeremiah 31:3*
If you will obey My voice, and keep My covenant, you will be Mine
own. *Exodus 19:5*
I know the plans that I have for you. *Jeremiah 29:29:11-14*

You will find Me if you will search for Me with all your heart and soul.
Deuteronomy 4:29
Delight in Me and I will give you the desires of your heart. *Psalm 37:4*
I will give you comfort. *2 Corinthians 1:3-4*

I will deliver the righteous from afflictions. *Psalm 34:19*
I will wipe away every tear from your eye. *Revelation 21:3-4*
I sent My Son to show My love for you, and save you. *1 John 4:8-12*

If you accept the gift of My Son, you accept Me. *1 John 3:23*
There will be great joy in heaven over one who accepts Me. *Luke 15:7*
I invite you, will you be My child? *John 1:12-13*

Love,
Your Forever Friend

Taken from the New American Standard Version of the Bible.

Acknowledgments and Thanks

~ *To our friends and family* who have seen me through this project, I appreciate you all more than you know.

~ *To Ann Gimbel* for getting me started on this project and for your helpful suggestions and encouragement. If not for you, this book would not have happened.

~ *To my children Debra and David and my granddaughter Kari* for typing the manuscript.

~ *To my granddaughter Bethany* for helping me figure out grammatical problems and build better sentences.

~ *To my husband, Everett,* for willingly sharing me with the computer and for reading my manuscript and offering suggestions. Your love and support are priceless.

~ *To my son Duane and his sons, Paul and Tom,* for bailing me out during my computer emergencies.

~ *To my daughter Diane and her husband, Jim,* for endless consultation and encouragement, suggestions, and computer counseling.

~ *To my daughter-in-law Linda* for her suggestions and ideas.

~ *To my daughter-in-law Bettina* for her help with makeup and outfits and for taking the original cover photography.

~ *To Emmett and Annette Koelsch* for letting us use their beautiful yard for the cover photo shoot.

~ *To Helen Zolber* for reading my manuscript and offering valuable suggestions and corrections—and thanks for a great recommendation for Duane to go to medical school all those years ago.

~ *To Ralph Winsor* for reading the manuscript and interviewing me on DVD. Also to his wife, Dereeta, and mother-in-law, Trudy, for reading the manuscript and for their encouragement.

~ *To Ruth Thompson* for her valuable editing help.

~ *To Dave Livermore* for taking time to read the manuscript, even while he was moving to a new pastorate.

~ *To Ruthie Jacobsen* for reading the manuscript and writing a preface. She has blessed my life more than she will ever know.

~ *To LifeScape Publishing's Ed and Eddie Schwisow* for their encouragement, project management, design consultation, editing, and proofreading.

~ *To Ron Burgard of MacMouser Graphics* for his design and layout skill and patience in getting the cover and its coloration "just right."

~ *To Matthew Rafano* for recording and preparing a companion DVD to *My Forever Friend.*

~ *To my son David* for his vocals and accompaniment on the DVD, and to my son Duane for recording and mixing the music track.

~ *To Alf Birch, Mardian Blair, Garland Edwards, and Gail Toney* for reading and endorsing the book.

~ *To all my dear friends* who have encouraged me, a big

"*Thank-you.*"

May God's name be glorified and praised!

Due to my deep interest in Christian education and Women's Ministries, I am willing to allow *My Forever Friend* to be used as a fundraiser. You may contact me with questions at:

1105 D 15th Avenue #435, Longview, WA 98632-3068
360-414-3246
email: roensfriend@gmail.com

~ To order more books, call: 1-800-247-6553 ~

Oregon Women's Ministries

A Ministry for every woman

Touch a Heart, Tell the World

"We have different gifts, according to the grace given us..." Romans 12:6

MISSION

Women's Ministries of the Oregon Conference has been established to:

†uphold women as they develop their unique God-given qualities,

†encourage their continued spiritual growth through prayer and Bible study,

†and equip them to fulfill the gospel commission.

RESOURCES

Women's Ministries Leadership Training; Camp Meeting Workshops; Christian Women's Retreats; Prayer Conferences; Mission Trips; and Support Groups for Widows, Divorced Women and Mothers.

CONTACT

Oregon Women's Ministries

19800 Oatfield Road

Gladstone OR 97027

Phone: 503-850-3500

Website: www.oregonconference.org, click on departments, and Women's Ministries.

"EVEN ON MY SERVANTS, BOTH MEN AND WOMEN, I WILL POUR OUT MY SPIRIT." ACTS 2:48

ALSO FROM ROEN:

THE AUTHOR OF MY FOREVER FRIEND

ROEN A. WILSON

Listen to Your
Heart

Finding the life partner of your dreams

Now that you've read Roen's life story in *My Forever Friend*, read *Listen to Your Heart*, a book where she shares with her grandchildren seven key areas in discerning if their "special someone" is life partner material. This 16-page wisdom-filled booklet is available at roensfriend@gmail.com, 360-414-3246.